The MAILBOX®

Year-R[illegible] Themes to Grow On

[illegible]es
[illegible]K–K

MW01051588

Over 300 Cross-Curricular Activities!

- Apples
- Pumpkins
- Farm animals
- Transportation
- Winter holidays
- Dinosaurs
- Insects and spiders
- Five senses
- Zoo animals
- And more!

16 popular classroom themes!

Managing Editor: Brenda Miner

Editorial Team: Becky S. Andrews, Diane Badden, Kimberley Bruck, Karen A. Brudnak, Bonnie Cave, Pam Crane, Lynette Dickerson, Sarah Foreman, Theresa Lewis Goode, Tazmen Hansen, Marsha Heim, Lori Z. Henry, Judy Huskins, Debra Liverman, Dorothy C. McKinney, Thad H. McLaurin, Sandy McNeil, Sharon Murphy, Jennifer Nunn, Mark Rainey, Laurel Robinson, Hope Rodgers, Donna K. Teal

www.themailbox.com

ISBN10 #1-56234-858-2 • ISBN13 #978-156234-858-8

Manufactured in the United States
10 9 8 7 6 5 4 3 2 1

Table of Contents

Activities at a Glance

Themes	Math	Language Arts	Science	Social Studies	Art	Snack	Other
Getting to Know You	4, 5	6, 7, 8	8	9, 12	10, 13	11	11
Safety	14, 22, 23	15	16, 22	17, 18, 19	20, 22	21	21
Apples	24, 25, 32	26, 27, 28, 32	29, 33	30	30	31	31
Five Senses	34, 35	36, 37	38, 39, 42, 43	39	40	41	41
Pumpkins	44, 45, 52	46, 47	48	49	50, 53	51	51
Farm Animals	54, 55, 62	56, 57, 63	58	59	60	61	61
Transportation	64, 65	66, 67, 72, 73	68	69	70	71	71
Winter Holidays	74, 75, 82, 83	76, 77	79	77, 78, 79	80	78, 81	81
Fairy Tales	84, 85, 92	86, 87, 93	88	89	90	91	91
Dinosaurs	94, 95, 102	96, 97	98, 99	99	100, 103	101	101
Pets	104, 105, 110, 111	106, 107	108	108	109	109	109
Spring Celebration	112, 113, 120	114, 115, 121	116	117	118	119	119
Over in the Meadow	122, 123, 130, 131	124, 125, 130	126	127	128	129	129
Insects and Spiders	132, 133, 140	134, 135	136, 141	137	138	139	139
Under the Sea	142, 143	144, 145, 150, 151	146, 150	147	148	149	149
Zoo Animals	152, 153	154, 155, 159, 160	156	157	158	158	158

Getting To Know You

Take a look at all of the fresh, new faces in your classroom. Each child has his own special, individual qualities to share with you and his classmates. These hands-on ideas and activities will help your children better understand and appreciate themselves and others.

MATH

Counting and Graphing About Us

Select a topic such as the number of boys/girls, hair colors, or eye colors. Gather the information to be recorded by brainstorming on that topic. For example, have your youngsters name all of the different colors of eyes that they know. Place a strip of each represented color on a bar graph and write the color word on the color strip. Have each child write his name on a construction paper square to represent himself on the graph. Count and tally the results of the various groupings and compare them.

Recipe for Measurement

Take advantage of class activities that can benefit from cooperation while also cooking up lots of fun! Pour a variety of snack foods such as goldfish crackers, cereal, and pretzels into individual containers. Place the containers in the center of a table. Assemble a small group of youngsters around the table. Give one child a measuring scoop. Tell him to choose one of the snacks and take one scoop of that food out of the container. Then have him pour the scoop of food into a large bowl. Record the ingredients for a recipe on chart paper as each child has a turn. Mix together the foods in the large bowl. Serve the mixture in paper cups as a snack and enjoy it!

Line Up!

Have several children stand in a line in front of the class. Name the child who is first, second, third, and so on. Ask the children to change positions. Then have each child in line name his new position. Repeat the activity using a new group of children. To vary the activity, have the children at their seats name each child in line and describe his position.

Positional Words

Have several students stand in front of the room. Give each youngster a verbal direction telling where to stand in relationship to the other students. Use positional words such as *beside, in front of,* or *between* to position the students. For example, "Donna, stand beside Jamie." To vary this activity, have the seated students give the children the verbal directions using positional words.

Measuring Up!

Organize children in groups of four. Give each child five strips of different-colored construction paper. Have each child use a different-colored paper strip to measure each part of his body. First have each child use a paper strip to measure around his head, cutting off the excess paper. Encourage each child to compare the length of his strip with those of the other children in the group. Glue each strip to a piece of personalized tagboard, making sure that the end of the strip is flush with the left-hand edge of the tagboard. Have the child label the strip by drawing the corresponding body part as shown. Repeat the same procedure for the neck, waist, wrist, and ankle.

Letter Counting and Sorting

Seat your youngsters around you. Encourage them to think of the first letter in their name. Hold up a flash card with a letter on it. Have each child whose name begins with that letter stand in a specific area of the room. Have one designated child in each group hold the letter flash card. Repeat these steps until all youngsters are standing in a group. Count the youngsters in each group and compare the total with the totals of the other groups. Invite your youngsters to determine which letter group has the most, the least, or the same amount.

LANGUAGE ARTS

The Howdy Hat

The Howdy Hat activity is an exciting way to introduce a variety of language skills and a rootin'-tootin' way to build self-esteem. To prepare for this activity, write each child's name on a strip of paper and place it in a cowboy hat. Pick one child's name from the hat. This will be your Howdy Hat child. Have youngsters ask questions to find out whose name was chosen from the hat. Encourage the youngsters to question such things as hair color, clothes the child is wearing, or the color of the child's eyes. Once the students have enough clues, have them guess the name of the Howdy Hat child. (Allow more questions if the guess is incorrect.) If the guess is correct, the Howdy Hat child should come to the front of the room.

Now it's time to lead your students in a cheer for the Howdy Hat child! For example, if the child's name is Donna, say, "Give me a D." The class would then respond, "D." Continue cheering each letter in the child's name. Finally say, "What does that spell?" and the class will respond, "Donna."

End the activity by encouraging your students to tell the Howdy Hat child what they like about her, keeping the comments very positive. Continue this activity each day until every child's name has been drawn.

The Name Game

Have the children sit in a circle on the floor. Hold up a beanbag and say, "My name is __________, and I like __________." Pass the beanbag to the child beside you and have him repeat the sentence, inserting his name and the thing he likes. Continue around the circle until everyone has had a turn. Then go around the circle again and have student volunteers try to retell each child's name and the specific thing he likes.

Interest Inventory

Type an interest inventory similar to the one below. Send a copy home with each child. Ask him to return the completed copy the next day. Collect all of the inventories and read each one to the class, omitting the name of the child. Then ask the children to guess which classmate is being described.

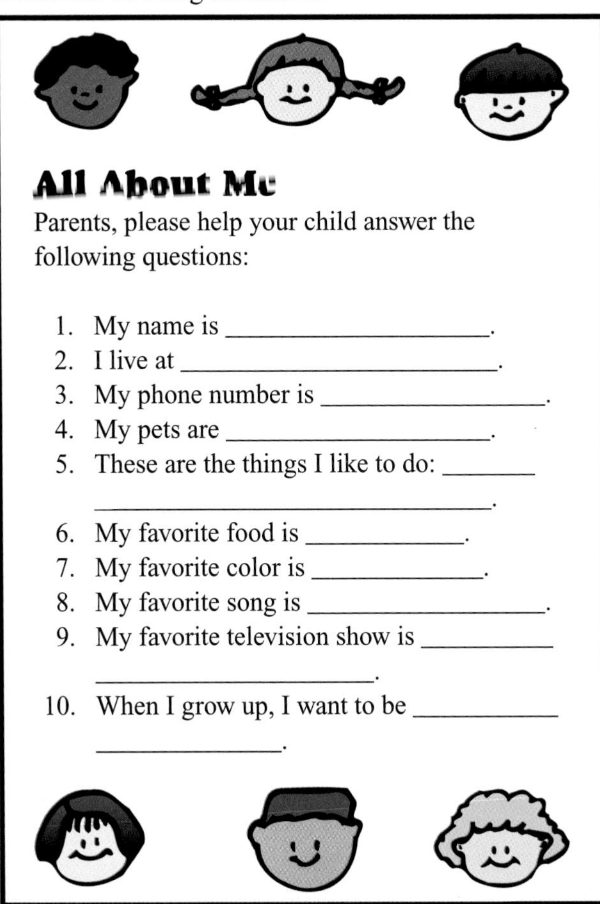

All About Me

Parents, please help your child answer the following questions:

1. My name is ____________________.
2. I live at ________________________.
3. My phone number is __________________.
4. My pets are ____________________.
5. These are the things I like to do: _______ ________________________________.
6. My favorite food is ____________.
7. My favorite color is _____________.
8. My favorite song is _________________.
9. My favorite television show is _________ _____________________.
10. When I grow up, I want to be ___________ ______________.

Smile for the Camera

Take a picture of each child in the classroom individually and then in a group setting. Glue both pictures on a sheet of construction paper. Below the individual picture, print the sentence "Hello, my name is ____________." Have each child fill in her name in the appropriate space. Below the group picture, print the sentence "Can you find me?" Then bind the papers together to create a class book. When the book is complete, share it with the students.

Handful of Fun!

Have each youngster trace one of his hands on construction paper. Then help him cut out the handprint. Encourage each child to think of two facts or interesting things about himself. Have him write or dictate for you to write these two things, printing one on the front and one on the back of the handprint. Have youngsters illustrate their sentences. These "hand-made" creations are great for sharing!

Five-Star General

Make a class chart with five spaces beside each child's name. Tell the children that for each of the following tasks they complete, they will receive a red star beside their names on the chart:

Name five classmates.
Name the teacher.
Name the principal.
Name the school.
Know your first name, last name, and phone number.

When a child completes all five tasks, place a gold star on his forehead and send home a note or certificate describing his accomplishments. Vary and increase the difficulty of the tasks as the year progresses.

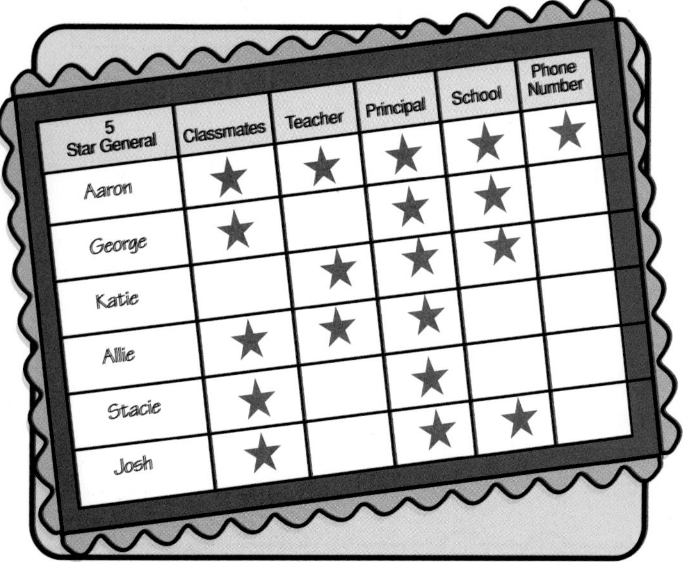

5 Star General	Classmates	Teacher	Principal	School	Phone Number
Aaron	★	★	★	★	★
George	★		★	★	
Katie		★	★	★	
Allie	★	★	★		
Stacie	★		★		
Josh	★		★	★	

Language Experience

Read aloud *Things I Like* by Anthony Browne. Have students discuss the things that the monkey liked and why. Then have each child think of one thing that she likes and have her complete the sentence "I like ______." Write each sentence on chart paper as it is dictated. Once all of the sentences have been recorded, copy each sentence on a separate sheet of paper. Give each child her sheet of paper and let her illustrate her sentence. Bind the papers together between construction paper covers to make a class book. Title the cover of the book "Things We Like!"

SCIENCE

Time Capsule

Supply each child with an empty potato chip can and a large piece of construction paper. Have each child decorate the construction paper and glue it to the can to create a time capsule. Then encourage each child to fill his capsule with personal items such as a picture of himself, an example of his handwriting, and a drawing. Replace the plastic lids and store the time capsules until the end of the school year.

A Classroom Garden

To enhance a spirit of cooperation and develop a sense of community among your students, make a class garden. To make a class garden, select an area on the school grounds for a garden. Have each child plant a daffodil or tulip bulb. Throughout the school year, assist youngsters in maintaining the garden.

To vary this activity, adopt a class tree already on school grounds. The youngsters can name the tree, make bird feeders for it, use its leaves for various classroom projects, and observe and record the tree's changes each season.

SOCIAL STUDIES

Faculty/Staff Introduction

Each day of the Getting To Know You unit, invite a faculty or staff member to spend time with your class. You may wish to invite the principal, school secretary, nurse, lunchroom personnel, or custodian. Encourage each guest to be prepared to talk to the class about her job responsibilities and to answer the youngsters' questions.

Class Directory

List each child's name in alphabetical order on a sheet of paper. Beside each name, list the child's address and phone number. Bind the list inside laminated covers to create a class directory. When a child needs a classmate's address or phone number, let him copy it from the book.

Me Booklet

Thrill your little ones with this booklet that is big on self-esteem. Reproduce page 12 on white construction paper for each child. Have children color and illustrate each page and then cut on the bold lines. Stack the pages, use a hole punch where indicated, and tie the pages together with yarn. Provide time for your youngsters to share the contents of their books.

Class Video

Enlist the help of a fellow teacher or an older child in the school to videotape your class during one of the first weeks of school. Have the volunteer videotape a portion of each of the daily activities in which the class is involved. Make a special decorated bag for the video. Then send it home with a child each night until everyone has had a turn.

ART

Self Collage

Tape a piece of paper to the wall. Place a lamp or overhead projector in front of the paper so that the light shines on it. In turn, have each child sit sideways in the light of the lamp. Trace the child's silhouette onto the paper. Cut out the silhouette. Have the youngster look through old magazines and cut out pictures of things that he likes. Students should then glue the magazine pictures in their silhouettes as collages. Please note that you may wish to have a teaching assistant or parent volunteer help you trace the silhouettes.

Friendship Sheet

Bring in a white, full-size sheet. Using a permanent marker, draw one large oval for each child around the perimeter of the sheet. Spread the sheet out on the floor. Have each child use bright-colored fabric paints to paint his face in one of the ovals. Once the fabric is dry, write the teacher's name, grade level, and room number in the center of the sheet. If desired, invite youngsters to use fabric paint to make handprints on the sheet between their faces and the printing. This friendship sheet makes a great display in any classroom.

Bulletin Board

Display the many patches of friendship in your classroom by making this friendship quilt. To make a quilt, cut several squares of brightly colored construction paper. Give each child one of the squares. Have him glue a photograph of himself in the middle of the square. Have each child decorate the remainder of the square with yarn, sequins, and glitter. Finally staple the squares, side by side, to the bulletin board to create a paper quilt. If extra squares are needed to fill the bulletin board, print information such as the school name or teacher's name on additional squares, and intermingle them with the students' squares as you staple them to the bulletin board.

Class Flip Book

Reproduce the paper doll outline on page 13 for each child. Have each child color the paper doll to resemble himself. Cut out the page on the top and bottom solid lines. Laminate each paper for durability. Bind the papers together to make a class book (spiral binding is best for this activity). Cut each page apart on the two solid lines. Encourage the youngsters to experiment by flipping the top, middle, and bottom sections of the book to create different combinations of people.

SNACK

Fruity Friendship Pizza

1 package slice-and-bake sugar cookies
1 package (8 oz.) cream cheese, softened
1 tub (8 oz.) whipped topping, thawed
sliced fruit (strawberries, bananas, peaches, pineapple)

Press the cookie dough into the bottom of a pizza pan. Bake it at 350° for 10 minutes. Blend the cream cheese and whipped topping. Spread the mixture over the cooled cookie crust. Add the fruit. Pour on the Orange Sauce (below).

Orange Sauce

Stir together the following ingredients:
½ cup sugar
dash of salt
1 tablespoon cornstarch

Gradually add these ingredients to the mixture:
½ cup orange juice
2 tablespoons lemon juice
¼ cup water

Cook the mixture until it thickens. Boil it for one minute. Pour it over the fruit. Slice and serve the fruit pizza.

CULMINATING ACTIVITY

Person to Person

Divide the class into pairs. Have partners face each other. Then name body parts that the partners must bring together. For example, you may call out, "Elbow to elbow," "Knees to knees," "Back to back," etc. Next call out, "Person to person," have everyone change partners, and begin the game again.

Getting To Know You Booklet

Use with "Me Booklet" on page 9.

Paper Doll Pattern

Use with "Class Flip Book" on page 10.

Safety

Stop, look, and listen! Use the following ideas to enable your students to take a big step toward learning the importance of safety in their everyday lives.

MATH

Parts of a Whole

Purchase a set of cardboard traffic signs from an educational supply store or enlarge a copy of the pattern from page 22. Laminate the signs for durability. Cut each sign apart to make a puzzle. Put all puzzle pieces in a box and place in a learning center. Have children in the center use the puzzle pieces to re-create the traffic signs.

Phone Home

Make a copy of the telephone pattern on page 23 and laminate for durability. Use a wipe-off marker to write the telephone number of each child in the rectangular shape at the bottom of a telephone pattern. Then write the numerals zero through nine on individual index cards and place in a box. Give each child the telephone with her phone number printed at the bottom and seven paper squares or buttons. Assign a student volunteer the task of being the telephone operator. Ask the operator to pick one numeral card at a time from the box and read it aloud. Let each child with that numeral cover it with a paper square or button. When a child has covered all the numerals in her telephone number, have her call out, “Hello.” Shuffle the numeral cards, choose another operator, and play again.

Matching

Make several copies of the safety signs on page 22. Color each sign and laminate for durability. Then cut apart individual safety signs. Put signs in a box and place the box in a learning center. Ask children in the center to match the signs that have the same shape or color.

Counting Order

Make a traffic light for each child in a learning center from a strip of black construction paper and glue on a red, a yellow, and a green circle. Then cut out several circles from white construction paper. Write a numeral on each white circle. Laminate traffic lights and paper circles for durability. Place sets of three sequentially numbered circles in individual bags. Have each child in a learning center place the set of numerals in counting order on a traffic light. One hint: to make the activity self-checking, color-code the back of each circle according to the order of the lights on a traffic light.

LANGUAGE ARTS

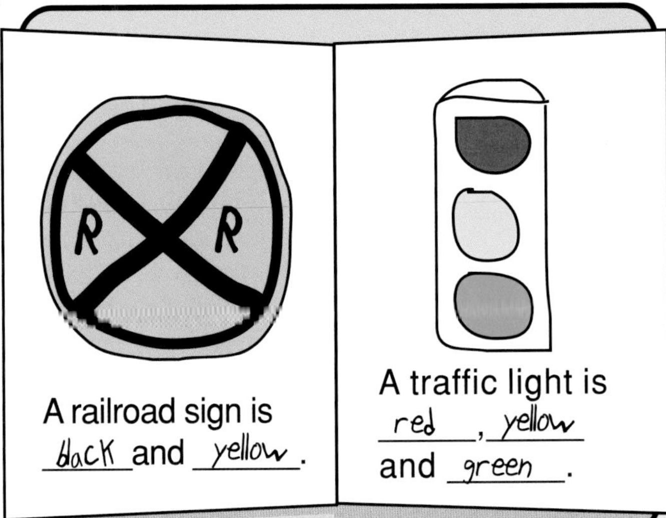

Signs, Signs!

Give each child a folded piece of construction paper to make a book cover. Have him trace or draw traffic signs on the cover. Each day, give him a sheet of paper with the sentence below printed at the bottom. Ask him to write the correct color words in the blanks. (Give younger children a resealable plastic bag with all the color words needed to complete the book. Write each word in the corresponding color. Have them select the appropriate words each day and glue them in the blanks.) Have each child draw a picture of the traffic sign above each sentence.

Monday—A stop sign is ________ and _________.
(red, white)
Tuesday—A yield sign is ________ and ________.
(red, white)
Wednesday—A hospital sign is ________ and ________. *(blue, white)*
Thursday—A railroad sign is ________ and ________. *(black, yellow)*
Friday—A traffic light is ________, ________, and ________. *(red, yellow, green)*

Brainstorming

Have children think of safety rules that apply to fire, water, traffic, home, and school. Write each set of rules on a separate piece of chart paper. Post charts in the classroom until the conclusion of the unit. Add new rules to the appropriate chart each day.

Safety Rules Are Cool

Each day, allow children to draw a picture of a safety rule being followed. Write the rule that each child's drawing illustrates on her picture. (Have older children copy the rule from one of the safety charts posted in the classroom.) Bind the pictures together to create individual safety books.

Vocabulary Words

Mount a large picture of a fire truck, firefighter, police officer, or police car on a piece of chart paper. Attach the chart to a wall or chalkboard. Have children take turns identifying or describing objects in the picture. Use a marker to write the name of each object on the chart paper. Then ask a child to draw a line from the word to the corresponding object in the picture. Conclude the activity by writing a sentence about the picture at the bottom of the chart.

SCIENCE

Fire and Air

Secure a candle in the bottom of each of two clean glass mayonnaise jars. Punch three or four holes in the lid of one of the jars. Making sure children are supervised, light the candles in both jars. Then place the lids on the jars. The candle inside the jar with the holes punched in the lid will continue to burn. The candle inside the jar with no holes in its lid will go out. Tell children that fire cannot burn without air. Then ask them to think about how a fire extinguisher might work and discuss it.

Hearing

Tape-record several warning and safety sounds (school fire drill alarm, smoke detector alarm, car horn, police whistle, etc.). Play the tape for the class. Help children identify the source of each sound. Then discuss the importance of knowing what to do when each sound is heard.

Lotto Sign Game

Duplicate the sign patterns on page 22. Choose nine of the signs. Color and mount these in a three-by-three configuration to form a lotto board. Duplicate four construction paper copies and laminate. Cut apart two of the copies for playing cards and reserve the other two intact for gameboards. To play the lotto game, have pairs of children stack the playing cards between them. Each child, in turn, draws a card and matches it to his board. The first to fill his board wins. If he chooses a duplicate card he puts it at the bottom of the stack.

To make a Concentration sign game, duplicate four construction paper copies as before, laminate, and cut them apart. To play, place all cards facedown and have students take turns turning over two cards, attempting to find the matching signs.

SOCIAL STUDIES

Safety Rules

Each day of the unit, focus on one area of safety, using the topics below and on pages 18 and 19. Included under each topic are basic rules to discuss and one or more activities designed to reinforce the discussion.

Fire Safety

1. Never play with matches.
2. If your clothing catches on fire, remember to stop, drop, and roll.
3. To avoid smoke, stay low and go.
4. Keep away from hot appliances.
5. Practice home fire drills.

Take the class on a field trip to a fire station. Arrange to have a firefighter give them a tour of the facility and discuss the importance of fire safety.

Water Safety

1. Never swim alone.
2. In a boat, stay seated and wear a life jacket.
3. Get out of the water during thunderstorms.
4. Walk around a pool.
5. Learn to swim.

Tell the class that they will play Water Safety Charades. First model play acting each water safety rule. Divide the class into pairs. Assign each pair a different water safety rule. Ask one child to pretend to be someone who is following the rule and the other child to pretend to be someone who is breaking the rule. Have the remaining members of the class guess which rule is being demonstrated.

Traffic Safety

1. Obey all traffic signs and lights.
2. Always fasten your seat belt.
3. Before crossing a road, look left, right, and then left again.
4. Listen and follow directions from the bus driver.
5. Keep both hands on the handlebars when riding a bike.

Arrange to have a school bus brought to your school. Have the driver describe the important safety features of the bus. Then ask him to discuss the proper behavior for children while riding a bus. Have the bus driver take your class on a short trip to practice the rules they have learned.

School Safety

1. Walk in the hallways.
2. Keep your hands and feet to yourself.
3. Keep litter in its place.
4. Stay alert and play safe on the playground.
5. Do not play with fire alarms or fire extinguishers.

Have a member of the school safety patrol or the principal come and talk to your class about school safety rules.

Take your class on a safety hunt throughout the school. Talk about safety in each of the following areas: the bus loading zone, hallways, stairways, playground, cafeteria, and classroom.

Home Safety

1. Know your home phone number and street address.
2. Do not take pills or medicine unless your parents give it to you.
3. Stay away from household cleaners.
4. Never open the door for strangers.
5. Attach emergency phone numbers near each phone in the house.

Describe several situations and have children tell what they should do. Listed below are a few suggestions.

- You left several toys on the stairs. Your mother is carrying a large load of laundry and has started walking down the stairs. What should you do?
- Your mother accidentally left the door open to the cabinet where the household cleaners are stored. You see your baby brother sitting beside the cabinet opening a bottle of cleaner. What should you do?
- You are at home and you hear the doorbell ring. You look out a window to see who is at the door, but you do not recognize the person. What should you do?
- While shopping at the mall you wander away from your parent and get lost. A security guard stops you and asks if she can help. What should you do?

ART

Mobile

Reproduce the safety signs patterns on page 22 for each child in a learning center. Have him color and cut out the signs. Then ask him to tape the end of a piece of yarn to the back of each sign. Tie the safety signs to a clothes hanger to create a mobile.

Thank-You Cards

Give each child in a learning center a sheet of paper and a straw. Drop a small amount of diluted tempera paint in the center of each sheet of paper. Ask each child to use his straw to quickly blow the paint across the paper. Repeat the procedure using different colors of tempera paint. Allow the paint to dry. Then have each child fold his paper in half to make a note card. Ask him to write a thank-you note inside the card to one of the resource people who visited the class during the safety unit. Mail all note cards to the respective visitors.

Safety Vehicles

Place an assortment of small boxes, containers of tempera paint, and several paintbrushes in a learning center. Let each child in the center choose a box. Ask him to paint the box to resemble a safety vehicle (police car, fire truck, ambulance, etc.). Then have him glue black cardboard circles to his vehicle for the wheels once the paint is dry.

School Bus

Draw a large school bus on yellow paper. Use black paint to color in the wheels, make stripes on the side, write a number on the front, etc. Cut around the outline of the bus once the paint is dry. Then cut a row of windows in the side. Attach the bus to a bulletin board or wall in the hallway. Then have each child paint or draw a picture of her face and cut it out. Place a few of the faces in each bus window. Then cover the windows with a piece of plastic wrap.

SNACK

Traffic Light Cookies

Make traffic light cookies in a small group setting.

slice-and-bake sugar cookie dough, softened
canned white frosting
red, green, and yellow food coloring

Roll out cookie dough that has been softened slightly. Cut out a 2" x 5" rectangle from the dough for each child in the group. Place dough rectangles on a cookie sheet and bake. Then divide the frosting into three containers. Add red, green, and yellow food coloring respectively to the containers of frosting. Have each child use a Popsicle stick to spread small circles of the frosting on her cooled cookie.

CULMINATING ACTIVITY

Safety Questionnaire

Give each child a copy of the safety questionnaire to take home and complete with the help of a parent. When the questionnaires have been returned, help the children to compare their responses.

Name ______________________________ Safety

Questionnaire

Fire	1.	Is there a smoke detector in your home?	❑ yes	❑ no
	2.	Has your family practiced a fire drill at home?	❑ yes	❑ no
Water	3.	Do you swim alone?	❑ yes	❑ no
	4.	Do you get out of the water during thunderstorms?	❑ yes	❑ no
Traffic	5.	Do you wear a seat belt when riding in a car?	❑ yes	❑ no
	6.	Do you wear a helmet when riding your bike?	❑ yes	❑ no
Home	7.	Do you know your home phone number?	❑ yes	❑ no
	8.	Do you know the emergency phone number?	❑ yes	❑ no
School	9.	Do you walk in the hall?	❑ yes	❑ no
	10.	Do you play safely on the playground?	❑ yes	❑ no

Safety Patterns

Use with "Parts of a Whole" and "Matching" on page 14, "Lotto Sign Game" on page 16, and "Mobile" on page 20.

Telephone Pattern

Use with "Phone Home" on page 14.

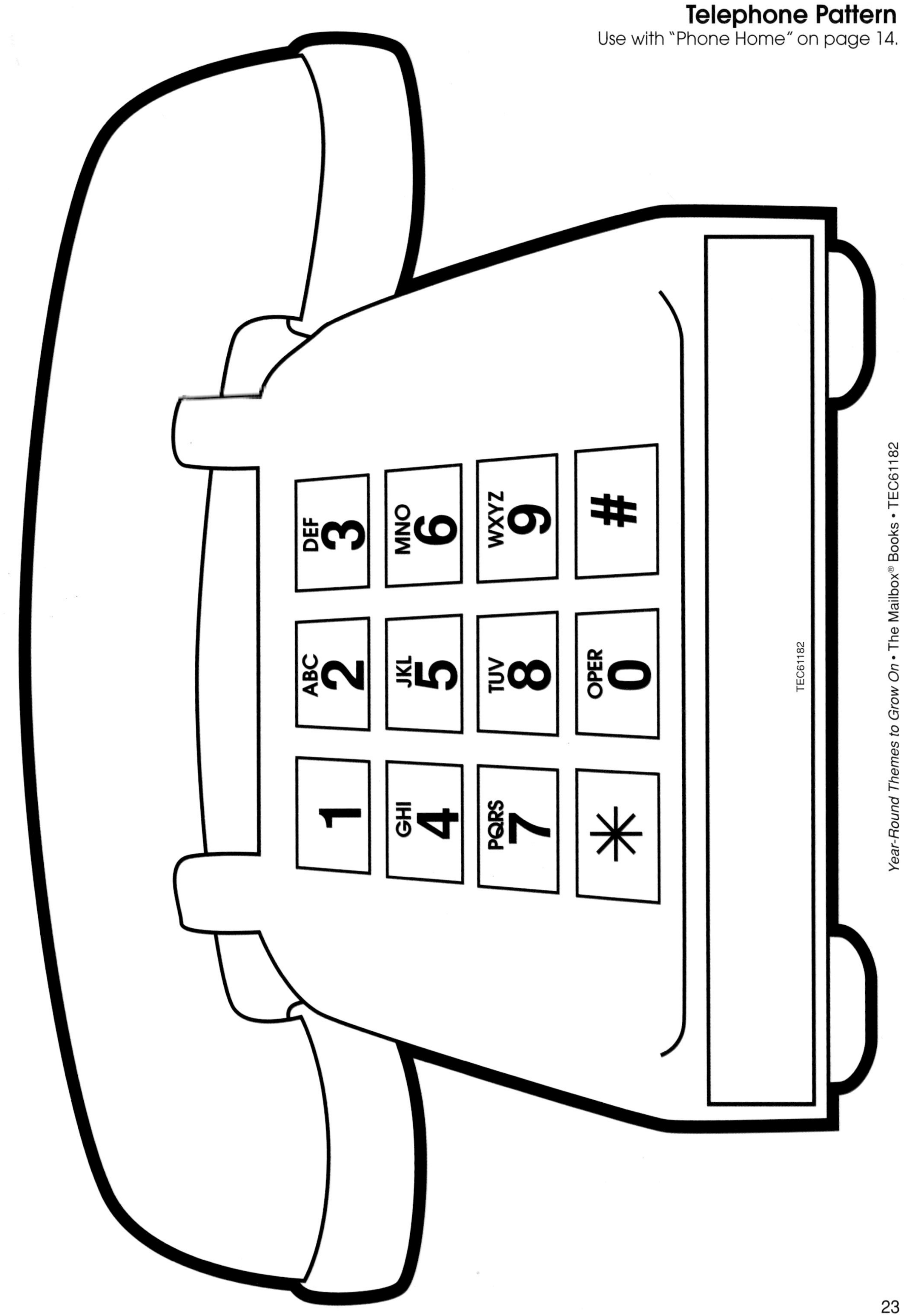

Year-Round Themes to Grow On • The Mailbox® Books • TEC61182

Apples

An apple a day turns work into play! Apple play in math, language arts, science, social studies, and art will keep your class smiling through the day. Bushels of fun-filled learning experiences await your youngsters as you bite into this "apple-tizing" unit on apples.

MATH

Counting With Apples

Duplicate the apple pattern on page 32 several times on red construction paper. Write a numeral and/or corresponding number word on each page. Laminate for durability. Place the apples and small containers of seed cutouts in a center. Have children place the correct number of seeds on each apple.

Sorting Apples

Ask each child to bring an apple to school. Put the apples in a bushel basket or box. Place the container of apples in a learning center. Have children sort the apples by color and size.

Estimation Apple Station

Give each child in a small group a piece of paper. Show him a red, a green, and a yellow apple. Have him use crayons to draw each of the three apples on his paper. Then encourage him to estimate the number of seeds in each one. Have him write the estimated number beside the appropriate drawing. Cut open the apples and have children count as you remove the seeds. Compare the number of seeds in each apple with children's estimations.

Apple Weighing

Place a set of scales, a cup of crayons, and an assortment of apples and another cup in a learning center. Ask children to weigh each apple, using the scales and several crayons. After each apple is weighed, have children count the number of crayons used. Let them determine which apple weighed the most, the least, etc.

More And Less

Use the apple pattern on page 32 to make several apples from construction paper. Punch a different number of holes in each apple, using a hole puncher. Place two apples side by side and have children count the number of "worm holes" in each apple. Then ask children to tell which apple has more worm holes and which apple has fewer. Repeat the activity using a different pair of apples.

Apple Seed Counting

In advance, put a blank sticker on the front of each of ten clean plastic jars. Then use a marker to write a numeral on each sticker. Place the jars and a container of apple seed cutouts in a learning center. Have children in the center put the correct number of seeds into the jars.

Apple Graphing

Make a large graph with drawings of a red apple, a green apple, and a yellow apple on the left-hand side. Attach the graph to a wall or board. Then show children examples of the three apples pictured on the graph. Ask children to sample a slice of each type of apple and describe how it tasted. Then let each child decide which apple he liked best. Give him a drawing of an apple. Let him color the drawing the color of his favorite apple. Have him cut out the apple and attach it to the graph beside the apple that matches his own. Conclude by counting the apples in each row and deciding which type was the most liked by the majority of the children.

Getting Your Apples In Order

Use the apple pattern on page 32 to make several apples from green construction paper. Write a different numeral on each apple. Laminate for durability. Attach a piece of felt to the back of each apple. Place two apples on a flannelboard. Ask children to tell which numeral would come before the pair and which would come after. Then place two new apples on the board. Have children tell which numeral would go between the pairs. Repeat the activity using different combinations of numbers.

LANGUAGE ARTS

Cooking Up A Recipe Book

Have children think of different foods that are made from apples. List the foods on chart paper. Then ask each child to bring a favorite apple recipe from home. Compile the recipes into a recipe book (include apple recipes used in the classroom). Make a copy for each child.

Beginning Sounds

Duplicate the apple pattern on page 32 several times on red construction paper. Cut each apple in half horizontally. Draw or paste a picture of an object on the top half of each apple. Then write the beginning sound for each object on the bottom half of the apple. Laminate for durability. Put the apple puzzles in a box. Place the box in a learning center. Have children in the center complete the puzzles by matching the objects to the beginning sounds.

Describing Apples

Make an apple booklet for each child in the class. Enlarge the apple pattern on page 32. Use the pattern to make a front and back cover from red construction paper. Staple three pieces of paper inside the cover. At the top of each page, write the sentence "Apples are ______." Next give each child an apple to observe and taste. Have him describe the various features of the apple (size, shape, color, weight, texture, etc.). List each of the descriptive words on chart paper. Then give him a copy of the apple booklet. Ask him to choose three of the descriptive words from the list. Have him complete the sentences by writing or dictating one of the words in each of the blanks. Let him use crayons to draw an illustration in the space below each sentence.

Storytelling

Below is a folktale about the star in the center of an apple. Tell the story to children, using a flannelboard and a figure of each of the characters in the story.

The Little Red House With No Doors

Once upon a time there was a little boy who was tired of playing with his toys. He said, "Mother, I am bored. What can I do?"

His mother said, "Go outside and find a little red house with no doors or windows and a star inside."

So the little boy went outside to search for the house. There he met a little girl. "Do you know where I can find a little red house with no doors or windows and a star inside?" he asked the girl.

"No, I don't," said the girl, "but my father may know."

So the little boy asked the girl's father, "Sir, do you know where I can find a little red house with no doors or windows and a star inside?"

The girl's father laughed and said, "No, Boy, I have never seen anything like that. Go ask Grandmother. She has lived a very long time and is very wise. Maybe she will know."

So the little boy asked Grandmother, "Please, can you tell me where I can find a little red house with no doors or windows and a star inside?"

"No," said Grandmother, "but I would like to find that house myself. Go ask the wind; he knows everything."

The wind blew by the little boy and the little boy asked, "Oh, Wind, do you know where I can find a little red house with no doors or windows and a star inside?"

The wind said, "Yes, Boy. I will show you the way." The little boy followed the wind up a grassy hill. At the top of the hill was an apple tree. The wind blew the tree and an apple fell off. "Look on the ground, Boy, and you will find your house," said the wind.

The boy looked on the ground and picked up the apple. "It's a little red house with no doors or windows, but where is the star?" asked the little boy.

The wind replied, "Take it home and ask your mother to cut it in half." The little boy hurried home to his mother.

"Mother, I have found the little red house with no doors or windows. Please cut it in half so that I might see the star." The little boy's mother took a knife and very carefully cut the apple in half. Inside was a star holding tiny brown seeds.

—Author Unknown

At the conclusion of the story, cut an apple in half horizontally and show the children the star.

Vocabulary Words

Draw three views of an apple (uncut, cut horizontally, and cut vertically) on a large poster board. Ask children to identify the different parts of the apples. Write the name of each part on the poster. Draw a line from the name to the corresponding part of the apple.

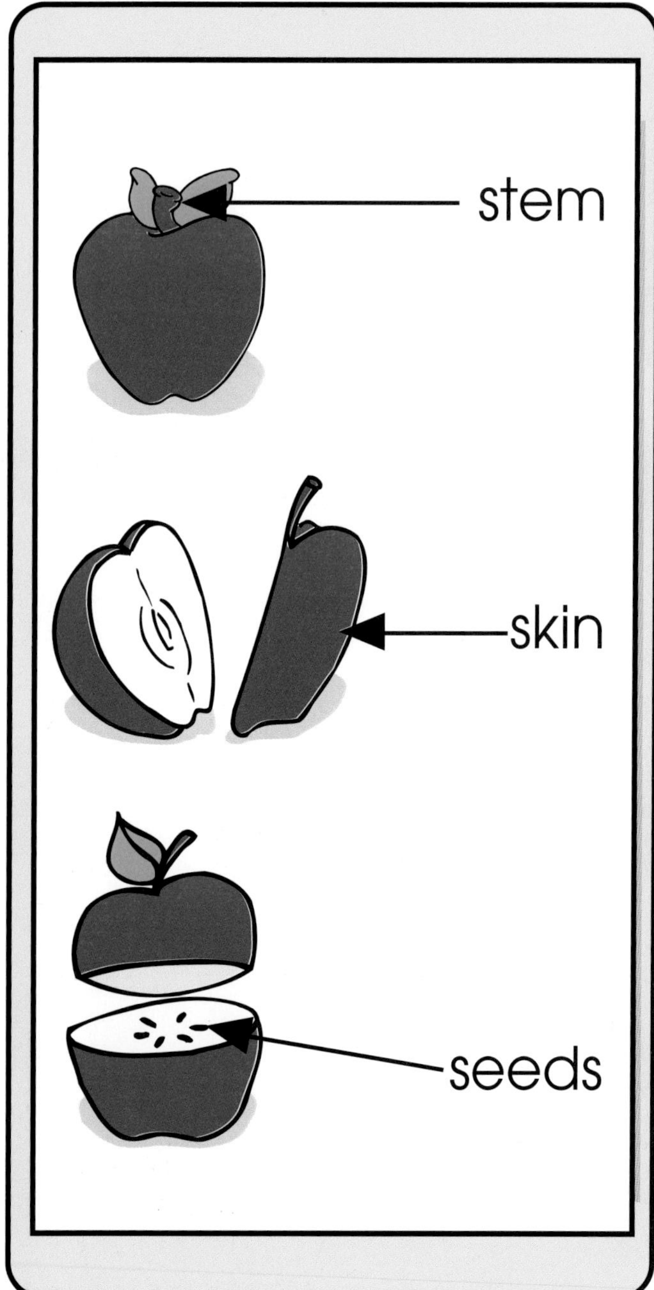

We Like Apples

Introduce this activity once the graphing activity on page 25 has been completed. Working in small groups, let each child complete the sentence "I like _____ apples," filling in the blank with the word *red, green,* or *yellow.* Write each sentence on chart paper. The next day, using the same small groups, let each child find her sentence on the chart. Read the sentence aloud. Then give her a strip of paper with her sentence printed on it. Ask her to cut apart the sentence, helping her to separate it between each word. Help her glue the words in the correct order at the bottom of a sheet of paper. Let her draw a picture of the apple she liked best on the paper above her sentence. Bind the papers together to create a class book.

SCIENCE

Graphing Apple Snacks

On each of the first four days of the apple unit, provide a different apple snack for children to enjoy. Listed below are suggested snacks.

Monday—raw apple slices
Tuesday—apple juice
Wednesday—apple butter or apple jelly on bread
Thursday—applesauce

Prepare a graph with a picture of each of the four snacks on the left-hand side. Give each child an apple cutout with her name printed in the center. Ask her to choose her favorite snack. Then have her attach the apple cutout to the graph beside the picture of the apple snack she liked best. Count the number of children who liked each of the four snacks and compare the amounts.

Sequencing

After discussing the growth of an apple tree, give each child a copy of the pictures on page 33. Have her color the pictures and cut them apart. Then ask her to glue the pictures in the correct sequence on a strip of construction paper.

Preserving Apples

Cut an apple in half. Rub one half with lemon juice. Do nothing to the other half. After a few hours, have children observe and compare the appearance of the two halves.

SOCIAL STUDIES

Community Workers

Contact the Agricultural Extension Service in your county to obtain the name of a person who works with apples and is willing to share his expertise with children. You also may wish to inquire about someone with an apple press who can make apple juice, someone who makes apple pies or apple turnovers, or an apple farmer.

Johnny Appleseed

Introduce children to the story of Johnny Appleseed by reading *Johnny Appleseed* by Patricia Brennan Demuth.

ART

Apple Printing

Cut two apples in half vertically and two in half horizontally. Place the apple halves in a learning center. Give each child in the center a piece of white construction paper and containers of red, yellow, and green tempera paint. Have him dip an apple half in the paint and make prints on the construction paper.

Sponge Painting

Give each child in a learning center a piece of white construction paper and a brown strip of paper. Have her tear along the edges of the strip to create a paper tree trunk. Ask her to glue the tree trunk in the center of the white construction paper. Next give each child a container of green tempera paint and a small sponge. Have her dip the sponge into the tempera paint and sponge-paint leaves above the tree trunk and grass below it. Then give her a container of red tempera paint. Have her dip a finger into the tempera paint and paint apples on the tree and a few below it.

Papier-Mâché

Have each child in a learning center crumple a piece of newspaper into a ball the size of an apple. Place several paper-towel strips and a container of papier-mâché mix in the center. Let each child dip paper-towel strips into the papier-mâché mix and use them to cover the ball of newspaper. Allow the papier-mâché apples to dry completely. Then let each child paint her apple with red, yellow, or green tempera paint. Insert a small stick into the top of the apple to make the stem. Then use a hot glue gun to secure the stick to the apple. Place completed apples in a large basket and use it as an attractive display in the classroom.

SNACK

Apple Snack

This is a nutritious apple snack that children will enjoy.

6 apples
prepared cinnamon oatmeal
(thick consistency)
chocolate chips

Wash and core the apples. Slice the apples horizontally. Have each child put a dollop of oatmeal on an apple slice and top it off with a few chocolate chips so it resembles apple seeds. Serves 12–18.

CULMINATING ACTIVITY

Conclude the unit on apples in the spirit of Johnny Appleseed. Have the children make apple bags for faculty and staff members. Give each child a brown paper lunch bag. Ask her to make an apple print on the front of the bag (see "Apple Printing" on page 30). When the paint has dried, let her place an apple and a note inside the bag. Then have her deliver the apple bag to a teacher or staff person.

Apple Pattern

Use with "Counting With Apples" on page 24, "More And Less" and "Getting Your Apples In Order" on page 25, and "Describing Apples" and "Beginning Sounds" on page 26.

Sequencing Pictures

Use with "Sequencing" on page 29.

Five Senses

Children will develop a heightened appreciation of the world around them as they see, hear, smell, touch, and taste their way through these "sense-sational" activities.

MATH

Counting (Hearing)

Have the children sit in a circle and count off by ones. Each child must listen carefully as the others count to know his number.

Counting Sounds (Hearing, Sight)

Ring a bell or clap your hands several times. Have the children listen for the number of sounds. Have them hold up their fingers to show how many times they heard the sound. Vary the activity by making two sets of sounds. Make one set of sounds, wait, and then make the second set. Have the children hold up their fingers to represent the total number of sounds in both sets.

Rhythm Patterns (Hearing)

Read aloud *Chicka Chicka Boom Boom* by Bill Martin Jr. and John Archambault to a small group of children. Give each child a musical instrument (maracas and/or drums). Have the children use the instruments to explore various musical patterns. Read the story again and have the children play the same musical pattern each time they hear the refrain "Chicka Chicka Boom Boom." Extend the activity by adding musical instruments or changing them. Then have the children make up musical patterns for songs such as "Mary Had A Little Lamb," "London Bridge Is Falling Down," or "B-I-N-G-O."

"Feely" Sock (Touch)

This made-in-a-minute Feely Sock is a great way for each youngster to explore her sense of touch. For each Feely Sock that you'd like to make, place several items of interesting texture or shape in a large plastic cup. Beginning at the bottom of the cup, slip an adult tube sock over the cup until the bottom of the cup is in the toe of the sock. To use the Feely Sock, a child slips her hand through the sock opening and feels the items in the cup. Add lots of variety to this activity by asking youngsters to describe what they feel, guess what they are touching, or retrieve a specific item without using their eyes.

Estimation (Sight)

Place several pom-poms in a plastic jar. Have each child estimate the number of pom-poms she sees in the jar. Record each child's estimate. Count the pom-poms in the jar to determine which child came the closest to the correct number.

Classifying (Touch)

Label each of four sheets of paper as shown with one of the following labels:

soft
hard
smooth
rough

Place objects representing each of the four categories in four separate shoeboxes. Label the boxes. Invite students to feel the different textures of the items.

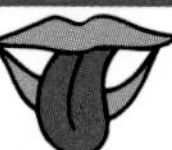

LANGUAGE ARTS

I Spy (Sight)

Put a twist on the traditional game of I Spy. Divide the class into four groups. Have a group of children look at one of the walls in the classroom. After a given amount of time, have the group members face away from the wall and name each of the objects they remember seeing. Repeat the process with the other groups. To vary the activity for a small group, have the children look at a detailed picture for a certain amount of time. Place the picture facedown and have the children name all of the things they remember seeing.

A Sensory Language Experience (All Senses)

Each child can make a "Five Senses" book he can read on his own. Select a different sense to write about each day of the unit. Give each child a sheet of paper with one of the following incomplete sentences printed at the bottom:

I can see a ________________.

I can smell a ________________.

I can hear a ________________.

I can taste a ________________.

I can touch a ________________.

Have each child dictate the word or words he wants written in the blank to complete the sentence. Older children may write the completion on their own. Have each child illustrate his sentence. At the end of the week, bind the pages together to make individual sensory books.

Listening To Letter Sounds (Hearing)

Have the children in a small group listen carefully as you say a pair of words. Have the children tell if the words sound the same at the beginning, or at the end of each word.

sheep—shoe (beginning)
dog—pig (end)

Story Sounds (Hearing)

Before reading aloud a familiar book to the children, assign specific sounds to certain characters or actions in the story. Have the children make the sounds at the appropriate points in the story.

Senses Signals (All Senses)

Read a familiar story, like "Goldilocks And The Three Bears," to the children. Have the children make the following signals each time one of the following words is read:

See or Saw—Make glasses with fingers around eyes.
Taste or Tasted—Stick out tongues.
Feel or Felt—Wiggle fingers.
Hear or Heard—Wiggle ears.
Smell or Smelled—Sniff noses.

Sound Toss (All Senses)

Label each of five shoeboxes with the name of one of the five senses. Place a few small plastic letters in each box. Put the boxes and a beanbag in a learning center. Have the children in the center take turns tossing the beanbag into a box. Have the child choose a letter from the box, say the sound it makes, and name something associated with the sense that begins with that sound. If a child chooses a *T* from the hearing box, he may say *trumpet.* If a child chooses *S* from the taste box, he may say *sandwich.*

Language Experience (Hearing)

Read *The Wheels On The Bus* adapted by Paul O. Zelinsky. Discuss the various sounds mentioned in the book. Have the children make a class book using the same format. The title might be "The Children In The Class." Sentences may be similar to the following:

"The clock on the wall goes tick, tick, tick, tick, tick, tick, tick, tick, tick. The clock on the wall goes tick, tick, tick all the school day long."

"The water in the sink goes drip, drip, drip, drip, drip, drip, drip, drip, drip. The water in the sink goes drip, drip, drip all the school day long."

Have the children work in pairs to write and illustrate one original sentence. Bind the pages together to create a class book.

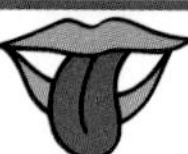

SCIENCE

Sight Box

Make a sight box to help the children understand that light is needed to help us see. Cover a shoebox with a secure-fitting lid. Use a pencil to punch a small hole in one end of the box. Cut out a two-inch-square opening from the center of the lid. Use a brad to attach a heavy piece of black paper to the lid so that it covers the opening and keeps out the light. Remove the lid and tape a small object to the bottom of the box directly beneath the opening.

Have the children experiment with the sight box in a small group. Cover the opening in the lid with the flap and have each child look through the hole. Then open the flap and have each child take another peek through the hole. Discuss with the children why they can see the object when the flap is open and cannot see it when the flap is closed.

Name That Tune

Children will enjoy experimenting with sound as they play Name That Tune. To conduct the experiment, use three identical glasses or glass jars, a metal spoon, water, and food coloring. Strike the empty glasses with the metal spoon. Have the children listen carefully to the sound. Pour water into each glass at a different level. Strike the glasses again and have the children listen carefully to the sounds. Add water to or pour out water from each jar to make the tones match the first three notes of the scale. Arrange the glasses by sound from lowest to highest. Place a few drops of red food coloring in the first jar, blue in the second jar, and green in the last jar. Have a child strike the jars with the spoon as you call out the following colors, or prepare a poster with the colors arranged in the correct order. Ask the children to name that tune once it has been played.

"Mary Had A Little Lamb"

green, blue, red, blue, green, green, green,
blue, blue, blue,
green, green, green.
green, blue, red, blue, green, green, green.
green, blue, blue, green, blue, red.

Extend the activity by adding jars dyed with other colors. Have the children play other familiar tunes or make up some of their own.

The Nose Knows

Make several smelly containers for this experiment. To prepare, collect the following supplies: opaque containers, pieces of gauze, smelly foods (an onion, coffee, a lemon, vanilla extract, cinnamon, peppermint extract, vinegar, an orange), and pictures of each food. Wrap each food item in a piece of gauze and place it in a container. Color-code the containers and corresponding pictures for easy checking. Have the children in a learning center open the containers one at a time and smell the contents. Then have the children match the pictures to the jars.

Tasting Party

Have a tasting party so the children can experiment with the sense of taste. Give each child a small plate with the following food items: pretzels (salty), marshmallows (sweet), dill pickle chip (sour), and unsweetened chocolate (bitter). Have the children taste each item, one at a time, and describe how it tastes. Give each child a copy of the recording sheet on page 42. Have him draw a picture of each of the foods he has tasted in the corresponding box.

Touch And Tell

Place a variety of objects in a "feely" sock (see "'Feely' Sock" on page 35). Have each child in a small group reach in the cup and feel one of the objects. Have him name three characteristics (such as *hard, smooth, slick, bumpy,* and *heavy*) of the object. Then ask him what he thinks the object is before he pulls it out of the cup. Continue the activity until everyone in the group has had a turn.

What's The Sense?

After each of the five senses has been discussed, have the children complete a copy of page 43.

SOCIAL STUDIES

Voice Identification (Hearing)

Tape the voice of each child in the classroom. Play the tape and have the children identify who is talking.

Community Workers (All Senses)

Invite a pediatrician, or a nurse, to visit. Ask her to talk about how she examines a child's eyes, ears, nose, and mouth. She may also discuss how to care for each of these important parts of the body.

Following Rules (Sight, Hearing, Touch, Smell)

People need rules to live together and keep our world safe. Our senses help us be aware of these rules and warn us of danger. Discuss how we use our senses to obey rules. For example, our eyes help us read rules such as traffic signs and warning labels. Our ears help us hear school fire alarms, car horns, and sirens. Our noses help warn us of potential dangers such as smoke and chemicals. After the discussion, have the children draw or cut out pictures from magazines of people using one of their senses to help them follow rules.

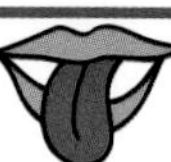

ART

Texture Collage (Touch)

Have each child bring in items of various textures (cotton balls, burlap, ribbon, sandpaper). Attach the items to a piece of poster board and place it in a learning center for the children to touch. Vary the activity by having the children classify the items by texture before attaching them to the poster board. If you do this variation, attach the items by classification to the poster board.

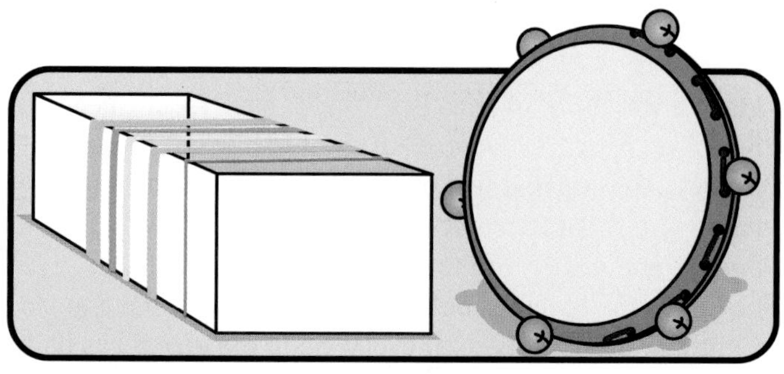

Rhythm Band Instruments (Sound)

Have each child make one of the rhythm band instruments featured, or let her invent an instrument of her own. Let the children use their completed instruments in a parade around the classroom or the school.

Kazoo—Paint a paper-towel tube. Stretch waxed paper over one end and secure it with a rubber band. Play by humming in the open end.

Rattle—Decorate a plastic bottle by applying tissue paper to the outside with liquid starch. Pour a handful of rice in the bottle, replace the lid, and shake it to play.

Tambourine—Use a hot glue gun to glue the rims of two plastic plates together. Use a hole puncher to punch holes around the rim approximately one inch apart. Have the child lace a piece of yarn through each hole, adding a large bell in six places. Shake the tambourine to play.

Rubber Band Instrument—Remove the lid from an empty shoebox. Cover the shoebox with aluminum foil. Stretch rubber bands of different widths and thicknesses around the center of the box. Play by gently strumming the rubber bands.

Shaker—Paint a toilet-paper roll. When it is dry, punch three holes around both ends of the roll. Use yarn or heavy string to tie large bells in each of the holes. Shake it to play.

SNACK

Soy Nut Butter Play Dough
(Touch, Smell, Taste)

soy nut butter
nonfat dry milk

Mix equal parts of soy nut butter and nonfat dry milk together until the dough is the consistency of play dough. Add more soy nut butter or dry milk as needed. Encourage the children to feel, smell, and taste the play dough as they use it to make various creations.

CULMINATING ACTIVITY

Five Senses Scavenger Hunt

Have your youngsters take a five senses scavenger hunt in your classroom. To prepare for a scavenger hunt, bring in several different items that easily lend themselves to the Five Senses unit. Write the name and a brief description of each item on a separate index card. Then show your students each of the items and discuss the various sensory characteristics of each one. Randomly place the items around your classroom. Then read aloud the description of each item from the index card. Have pairs of children try to locate the item that is being described. Below are some suggested items and descriptions for the scavenger hunt. Happy hunting!

- something that tastes sour (lemon)
- something that is rough to touch (sandpaper)
- something that is pleasant to smell (flower)
- something that tastes sweet (honey)
- something that makes a loud sound (horn)
- something that makes a ticking sound (a clock)
- something that feels soft (cotton)
- something that looks colorful (a picture of a rainbow)
- something that smells spicy (cloves or cinnamon)
- something to look through or read (a book)

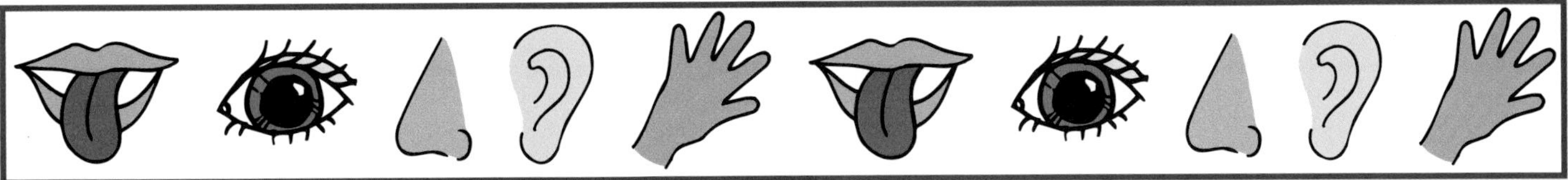

Name ____________________

"Sense-sational" Science

 Note to the teacher: Use with "Tasting Party" on page 38.

Name ____

What's The Sense?

Year-Round Themes to Grow On • The Mailbox® Books • TEC61182

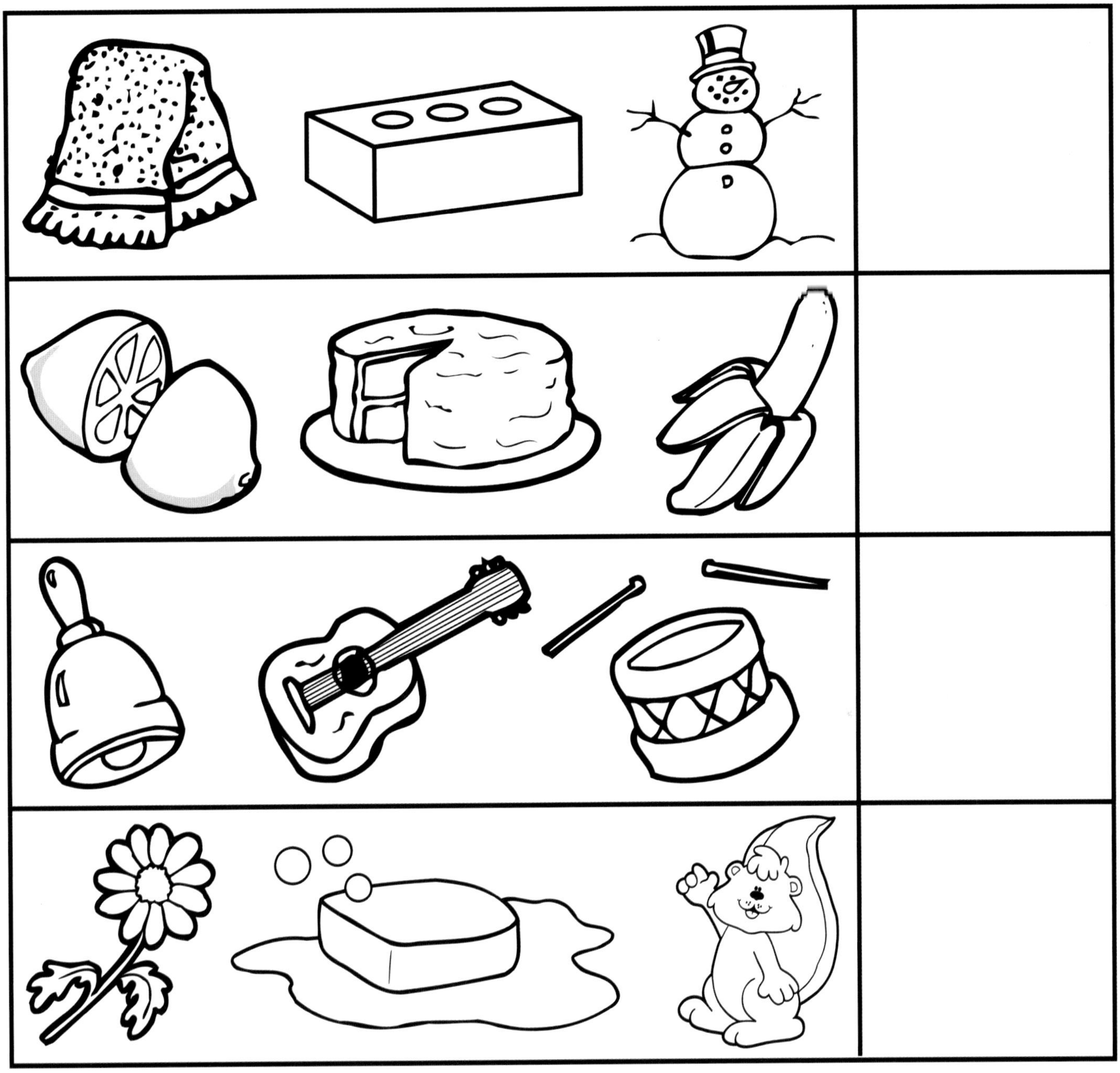

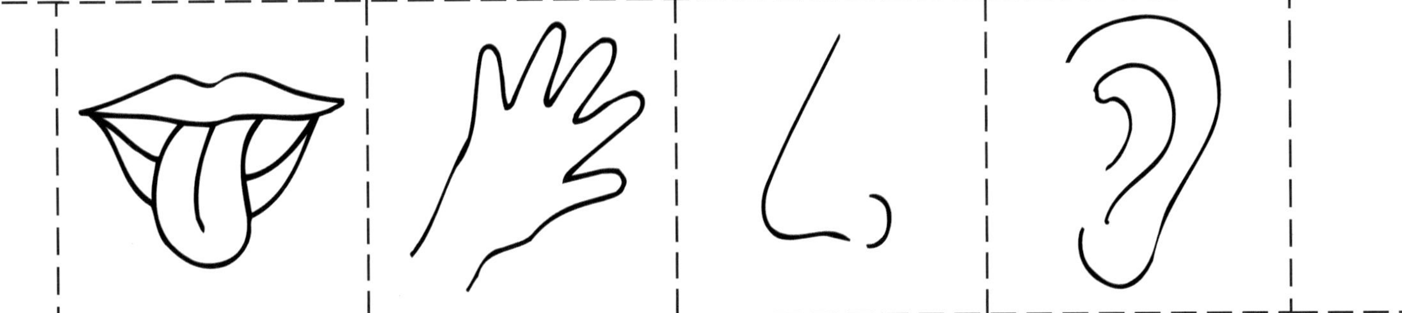

Note to the teacher: Use with "What's the Sense?" on page 39.

Pumpkins

Tiptoe through the pumpkin patch and harvest a roomful of centers and activities that extend learning and promote cooperation.

MATH

Pondering Pumpkins

Cut open a pumpkin and let the children look inside at the many seeds. Ask each child to estimate the number of seeds he sees. Record each response on chart paper or on a large pumpkin cutout. Count the pumpkin seeds to see who had the closest estimate.

Prize Pumpkins

Demonstrate how to measure pumpkins of various sizes by using a ball of string. Hold one end of the string on the pumpkin. Wrap the string around the pumpkin. Cut the string at the point where the two ends meet. Hold up the string so the children can see its length. Then show the children another pumpkin. Have each child estimate the size of the pumpkin by cutting a piece of string that he thinks is long enough to go around the widest part of the pumpkin. Have each child use his string to measure the actual size and then tell if his estimation was longer or shorter than the actual size.

Weighing Pumpkins

Let each child hold a pumpkin and estimate its weight. Record each child's estimate on chart paper. Place each pumpkin on a bathroom scale to find out its exact weight. Compare the exact weight with each estimate. Discuss how many estimates were less than the actual weight of the pumpkin and how many were more.

Mr. Jack-O'-Lantern

Draw one-half of a jack-o'-lantern face on a sheet of paper. Make a copy for each child. Have children complete the picture by drawing the missing parts of the face to match the other side.

Pumpkin Problem Solving

Make up several word problems related to pumpkins that are similar to those listed. Write them on large pumpkin cutouts. Read each word problem aloud and have student volunteers use pumpkin cutouts to solve each problem.

David has 3 pumpkins. Jessica has 3 pumpkins. How many pumpkins do they have in all?

The pumpkin farm sold 5 pumpkins before lunch and 4 pumpkins after lunch. How many pumpkins were sold in all?

Michael had 6 pumpkins. He gave Natalie 2 pumpkins. How many pumpkins does Michael have left?

Keesha has 4 pumpkins. Ann has 2 pumpkins. How many more pumpkins does Keesha have than Ann?

Sequencing

Give each child a copy of the pumpkin cards on page 52. Have him color each pumpkin and cut the pictures apart on the solid lines. Have him glue the pumpkin pictures in the correct sequence on a strip of construction paper and then number the pictures sequentially from one to six.

Counting

Prepare a supply of number cards labeled 1 through 10, along with a supply of pumpkin cutouts. Place the cards facedown in a pile. In turn, each child chooses a card and identifies the number. Then he counts out the corresponding number of pumpkin cutouts. After confirming that the number of pumpkins counted is correct, have him place his card to the side and return the pumpkin cutouts. The game ends when all the cards have been drawn. For older students, have them choose two cards and count the total number of pumpkins.

LANGUAGE ARTS

A Pumpkin Story

Read aloud the book *Pumpkin Pumpkin* by Jeanne Titherington. Have the children create individual books with a similar format. Type or print the sentences listed below on a sheet of paper and make a copy for each child.

1—Jamie planted a pumpkin seed.
2—The pumpkin seed grew a sprout.
3—The pumpkin sprout grew a plant.
4—The pumpkin plant grew a flower.
5—The pumpkin flower grew a pumpkin.
6—The pumpkin grew and grew until he picked it.
7—Jamie carved a pumpkin face.
8—He saved six pumpkin seeds for planting in the spring.

Cut the sentences apart. On each day of the unit, read aloud the sentences printed on the strips. Have each child glue the sentence strips on separate sheets of paper and illustrate each page. Add a special touch to the book by cutting the pages and the cover in the shape of a pumpkin.

Pumpkin Relatives

Pumpkins belong to the same family as gourds, squash, watermelons, cucumbers, honeydew melons, and cantaloupes. Have the children compare the similarities and differences between a pumpkin and each of the other family members. Have the children hold and observe each of the samples. A picture may be substituted if the actual item is not available. Divide a sheet of chart paper in half. Label one side "Same" and the other side "Different." Have the children discuss similarities and differences as you list them under the appropriate heading.

Positioning Pumpkins

Give each child a sheet of paper and some crayons. Ask her to listen and watch carefully as you describe and demonstrate where to draw five different pumpkins on the sheet of paper.

Draw an orange pumpkin in the top right corner.
Draw a green pumpkin in the bottom right corner.
Draw a yellow pumpkin in the center of the paper.
Draw a red pumpkin in the bottom left corner.
Draw a blue pumpkin in the top left corner.

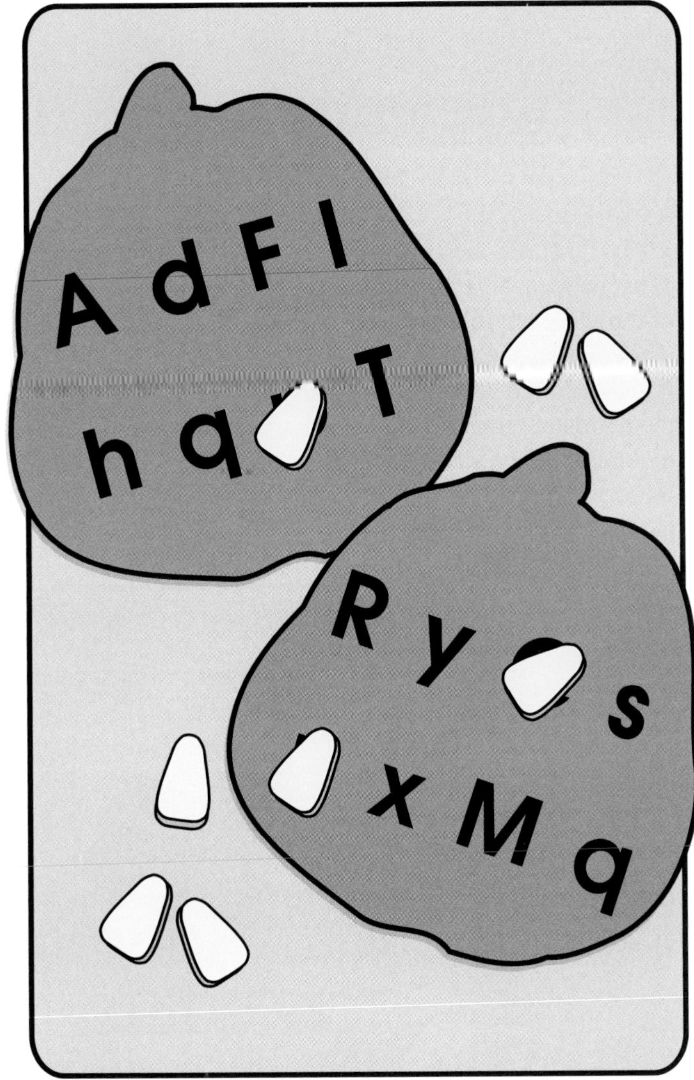

Grow, Pumpkin, Grow!

Read *The Biggest Pumpkin Ever* by Steven Kroll and "The Garden" from *Frog And Toad Together* by Arnold Lobel. Have the children brainstorm some things they could do to help a pumpkin grow to become large. Encourage them to use their imaginations, even though many of the suggestions may be unrealistic. Write the suggestions on a sheet of chart paper as they are dictated by the children. Copy each child's sentence on a sheet of paper and have him illustrate it. Older children may copy their own sentences from the chart paper. Bind the pages together to create a class book titled "How To Grow A Big Pumpkin."

Letter Recognition

To prepare for this activity, make several pumpkin cutouts from large sheets of orange construction paper. Use a marker and write a different set of upper- and lowercase letters on each pumpkin to create a gameboard. Place the gameboards, a set of alphabet cards, and a container of candy corn cutouts in a learning center. Give each child a gameboard. Place the alphabet cards facedown in the center of the playing area. Turn the cards over one at a time and call out the name of the letter on each card. If a letter appears on a child's gameboard, ask her to cover it with a piece of candy corn. Continue until each child completes her gameboard.

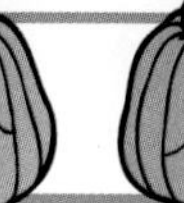

SCIENCE

Sequencing Foldout

The children will enjoy making simple fold-out books that show the growth sequence of a pumpkin. Cut several 6" x 18" strips of paper. Fold each strip in four equal sections. Label the sections in order: "Seeds," "Vine," "Flowers," "Pumpkins." Give each child one of the fold-out books and ask him to illustrate each section.

Sprouting Indian Corn

Discover more about another harvesttime crop while learning and experimenting with Indian corn. Place an ear of Indian corn in a shallow container of water (a foam tray works well). Check the container each day to make sure there is water in the bottom. The corn should begin to sprout in about one week.

Pumpkin Changes

What happens to a pumpkin after Halloween? Instead of throwing out the class jack-o'-lantern, keep it in the classroom in a sealed container and observe the changes it goes through as it rots. Have the children check the pumpkin regularly and take photographs or draw pictures to display on a timeline to record the changes. Some changes to look for are the following: mold, differences in colors, changes in shape.

SOCIAL STUDIES

Cooperative Pumpkin Games

Use these pumpkin games to develop cooperation and sportsmanship among the children.

Pumpkin Over And Under—Divide your youngsters into two lines for relay teams. In each line, have team members space themselves one arm's length apart. Give the first child in line a beach ball, a playground ball, or an orange Nerf ball. After the signal is given, the first child passes the ball over his head, the next child gets the ball, and he passes it between his legs to the next child in line. The ball is passed over and under until it reaches the last child in line. The last child takes the ball, runs to the front of the line, and continues the game. Play continues until the first child is once again at the beginning of the line. For younger children, have each child pass the ball either over their head or between their legs.

Pumpkin Relay—Fill two pumpkin lawn bags with leaves or crumpled newspaper, and seal them. Have the first child from each of the two relay teams roll one of the bags to the opposite end of the playing area and back. Continue until all the members of the teams have had a turn. The team that finishes first wins the relay.

A Pumpkin Patch Trip

Contact a pumpkin farm in your area to arrange a field trip for your class. The children will be given a tour of the facilities and in some cases will be allowed to choose small pumpkins to take back to school.

ART

Patches Of Pumpkins Bulletin Board

Have each child participate in the creation of a classroom pumpkin patch. Have a small group of children paint several large sheets of paper with green finger paint. When the paint dries, cut out a long vine and several leaves from the paper. Attach these to a bulletin board. Have each child use a sheet of orange construction paper and a small piece of black construction paper to create a torn-paper jack-o'-lantern. Tear a black jack-o'-lantern face and glue it onto a torn orange pumpkin. Glue a small sponge square to the back of each jack-o'-lantern before attaching it to the bulletin board. This will give your pumpkin patch a 3-D effect.

Scarecrow

A scarecrow is always a welcome addition to any pumpkin patch. Have the children make simple scarecrows using the reproducible patterns on page 53. Make several patterns out of tagboard. Use the shirt pattern to make cloth shirts from burlap. Place the tagboard patterns, burlap shirts, colored construction paper, small fabric scraps, scissors, glue, crayons or markers, and craft sticks in a learning center. Have each child use the pattern pieces to trace and cut out the parts of the scarecrow. Have him glue the parts together and attach a burlap shirt over the paper shirt. Have him glue the fabric scraps to the scarecrow's clothing. Have each child cut small, thin, construction paper strips and glue them randomly on the scarecrow so it resembles straw. Have each child use crayons or markers to draw the scarecrow's face. Finally glue a craft stick to the back of each scarecrow.

Tissue-Paper Pumpkins

Give each child two sheets of orange tissue paper and a lightweight hanger bent into a circular shape. Have him place the hanger on one sheet of the tissue paper so the hook extends past the top of the paper. Then let him glue around the inside and outside edges of the hanger. Next ask him to place the second sheet of tissue paper on top of the hanger and to press the two sheets together with the hanger in between. When the glue dries, trim the tissue paper close to the hanger. Next let the child use construction paper scraps to create features for the pumpkin. Then hang the pumpkins on prepared vines in the classroom.

SNACK

Crustless Pumpkin Pie

¾ cup sugar
½ cup Bisquick mix
2 tablespoons margarine
1 can (13-oz.) evaporated milk
2 eggs
1 can pumpkin (approximately 2 cups)
2½ teaspoons pumpkin pie spice
2 teaspoons vanilla

Mix all ingredients and beat until smooth. Pour the mixture into a greased pie tin. Bake at 350° for 50 to 55 minutes. Vary the recipe by pouring the mixture into small muffin tins. Bake at 350° for 25 to 30 minutes.

CULMINATING ACTIVITY

Decorated Pumpkins

Have each child decorate a pumpkin to enter in a decorated-pumpkin contest. Prepare a certificate for each child who enters the contest and prepare ribbons for the first-, second-, and third-place winners. Enlist the help of fellow staff members to serve as judges for the contest. Display the decorated pumpkins in the school lobby or media center.

Pumpkin Patterns

Use with "Sequencing" on page 45.

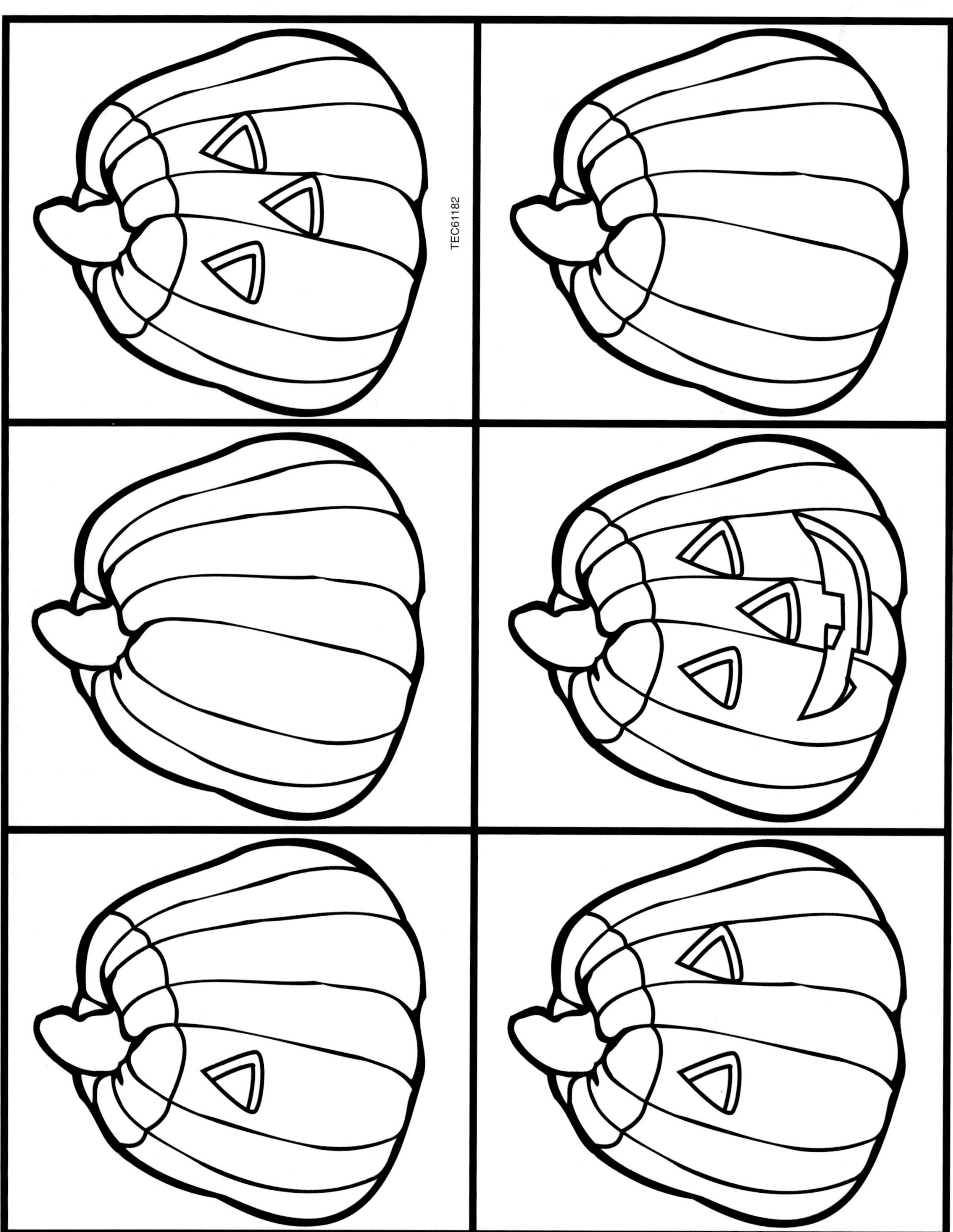

Scarecrow Patterns

Use with "Scarecrow" on page 50.

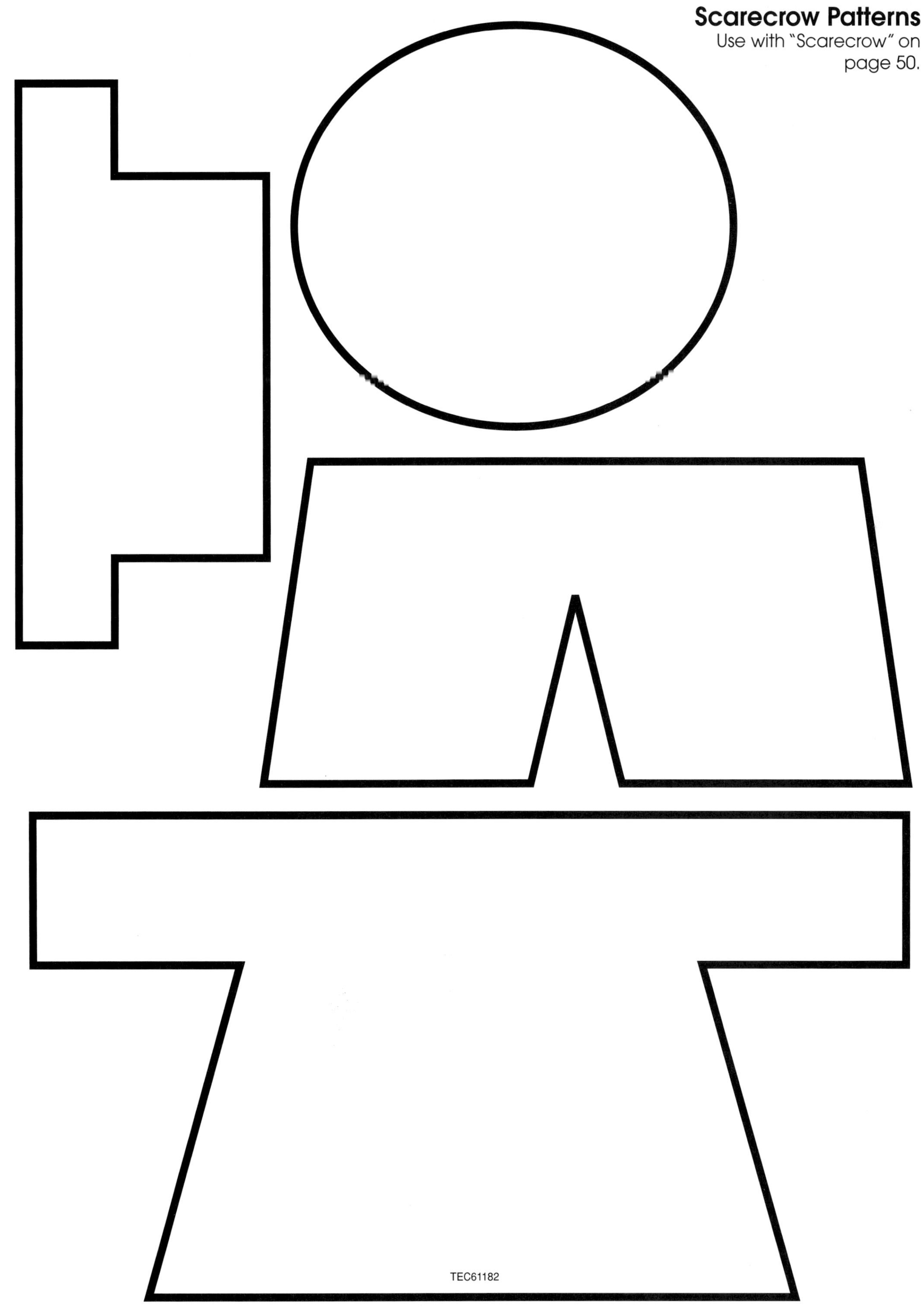

Farm Animals

Put on your best overalls, join the hayride, and travel the dusty roads to a farm. A barnyard filled with animal sights and sounds awaits you at the end of the journey.

MATH

Counting Critters

Make several copies of the farm animal cards on page 62. Mount the cards on tagboard. Then make a set of numeral cards using the numerals 1 through 9. Place the cards in a learning center. Have each child in the center choose a numeral card and place the appropriate number of farm animal pictures beside it. To vary the activity, use plastic farm animals instead of the farm animal cards.

To Market, To Market!

Set up an egg market in your classroom with plastic eggs, several craft foam pennies, and a large basket. First put a blank sticker or a small piece of tape on each egg. Then use a permanent marker to write a price on each egg, and place the eggs in the basket. Place the basket in a learning center. Give each child in the center ten foam pennies to use at the egg market. Tell him that he must spend all ten of his pennies when purchasing eggs. Then let him make his choices. When everyone in the center has had a chance to shop for eggs, have the children compare their purchases to see who got the most for his money, who got the least, etc.

Weight

Reproduce the farm animal cards on page 62. Color the animals and attach the cards to a sheet of tagboard. Laminate and cut apart the individual cards. Glue a piece of felt to the back of each card. Place two cards side by side on a flannelboard. Encourage children to look at the pictures of the animals. Have them tell which animal would weigh the most and which would weigh the least. Repeat this with different combinations of cards.

Animal Patterning

Use the duplicated farm animal cards made for the "Counting Critters" activity on page 54 to play a patterning game. First have children in a small group sit in a semicircle. Then place all of the cards faceup in front of the children. Begin a simple pattern by selecting a few of the cards and placing them in a line. Have children in the group take turns adding cards to the line to make a pattern. Repeat this procedure, creating several new patterns. Then let children use the cards to make original patterns.

Ordinal Positions

Make ribbons similar to those awarded to winners at a county fair (the color of each place winner is listed below). Then make a poster listing the ordinal positions first through fifth. Beside the word for each ordinal position, glue a piece of ribbon of the appropriate color. Attach the poster to a wall or board. Review the ordinal positions and ribbon colors with the children. Then have five children stand in a line and pretend that they are winners at a county fair. Ask the children remaining at their seats to tell which child would receive the red ribbon, yellow ribbon, etc. As each child is named, give her the appropriate ribbon. Repeat the activity using a different group of children.

first—blue
second—red
third—green
fourth—pink
fifth—yellow

LANGUAGE ARTS

Listening

Set up a listening center in the classroom using a taped reading of *The Little Red Hen.* Give each of the children in the center a copy of the book *The Little Red Hen.* Ask him to follow along in his book as he listens to the tape. Then have children act out the story (simple masks representing each of the characters in the story may be used). Conclude by providing the group with a small loaf of bread to be sliced and served to each child.

Wishy-Washy Language Experience

Read *Mrs. Wishy-Washy* by Joy Cowley. Then ask children to think of other farm animals that might have been included in the story. Write the name of each animal on a sheet of chart paper. Next have children dictate a story about Mrs. Wishy-Washy that includes most of the animals on the list. Ask children to follow the format of *Mrs. Wishy-Washy.* Rewrite each sentence on a separate sheet of construction paper. Have each child illustrate a sentence and bind the pages together to create a class book. Record the original story *Mrs. Wishy-Washy* on one side of a cassette tape. Then have the children record their version on the other side of the tape. Place the tape, copies of *Mrs. Wishy-Washy,* and the class book in a listening center.

Clipping Beginning Letters

Use a marker to divide a cardboard circle into eight sections. Glue a picture of a different farm animal in each section. Write the beginning letter of each animal on an individual clothespin. Have a child in a learning center clip each clothespin to the part of the wheel picturing an animal with the name that begins with that letter. *(Note: The clothespins and the back of the circle may be color coded to make the activity self-checking.)*

Sequencing

Read *Hattie And The Fox* by Mem Fox.
Discuss the sequence of events in the story. Then give each child a copy of the cards on page 63 and have her cut them out. Assist the children as they correctly sequence the pictures on a strip of construction paper. Have them glue the pictures in place.

Dramatic Play

Read *Big Red Barn* by Margaret Wise Brown. Then have child volunteers act out the story while the remaining members of the class reread the book.

A Walk With Rosie

Read *Rosie's Walk* by Pat Hutchins to a small group of children. Point out each of the position words used in the story *(across, around, over, past, through,* and *under*). Then have children follow you on a course set up in the classroom that is similar to the one taken by Rosie. Listed below are some suggestions for the course layout.

across the yard—Walk across the floor.
around the pond—Walk around a piece of blue paper placed on the floor.
over the haystack—Walk over a small stool or wooden box.
past the mill—Walk past a door.
through the fence—Walk between two chairs.
under the beehives—Crawl under a table.

SCIENCE

Farm Animals

Introduce children to farm animals and their young by reading *Baby Farm Animals* by Garth Williams.

Animal Products

Make poster board cutouts of a cow, sheep, goose, and chicken. Have children discuss various products derived from each of the four animals. Then let each child look through an old magazine. Ask him to cut out pictures of some of the products mentioned in the discussion. Glue each of the pictures to the animal cutout.

Making Butter

Give each child in a small group a clean plastic jar. Pour one-fourth cup of whipping cream into the jar. Secure the lid tightly. Have her vigorously shake the jar until the cream solidifies into butter. Serve the homemade butter on crackers and enjoy them. Hint: The butter will form faster if the jars are refrigerated to make them cold before using.

SOCIAL STUDIES

Field Trip

An excellent way to acquaint children with farm animals is to take them on a field trip to a local county fair or an animal farm equipped to handle visitors.

Farming Fun

Draw a map of a farm on a large sheet of paper (include a barn, silo, pond, pigpen, chicken coop, pasture surrounded by a fence, garden, road, and farmhouse). Place the map and several small plastic farm animals in a learning center. Let the children in the center play with the farm set, placing the animals in various locations on the map.

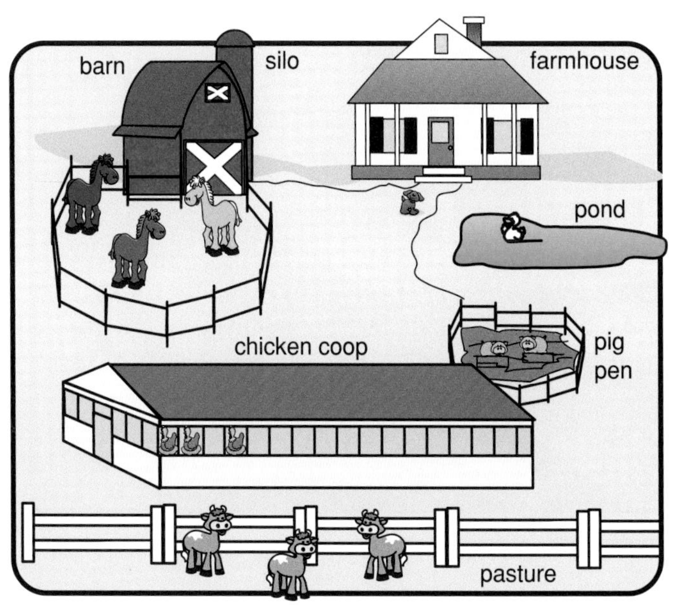

Farm Animal Trivia

List the names of several male, female, and baby farm animals on a sheet of paper (such as sow—female pig, gander—male goose, piglet—baby pig, etc.). Call out the animal names one at a time. Have children identify each name by describing the animal.

Farm Workers

Contact the Agricultural Extension Service or a local 4-H representative to find people willing to talk to your class about the various jobs on an animal farm.

Dairy Farm

Read *The Milk Makers* by Gail Gibbons. Then take children on a field trip to a dairy farm. Take several photographs of different parts of the farm. Glue each of the photos on a different sheet of paper and write a caption below each one. Bind the papers together to create a class book. To vary this activity, have each child draw a picture of his favorite part of the dairy farm. Have him write or dictate a sentence for you to record, describing his picture. Bind the papers together to make a book.

ART

Shoebox Diorama

Invite each child to create a farm scene inside a shoebox. The background can be colored with markers or painted. Toy farm animals and fences can be used along with straw, grass, or similar materials. A barn, silo, chicken coop, and farmhouse may be drawn on separate pieces of paper and attached to the sides of the shoebox. Ask each child to share her shoebox diorama with the class. Then place the dioramas on display in the classroom, space permitting.

Bulletin Board

Cover a large bulletin board with a farm scene. To do this, staple a piece of light blue paper to the top of the bulletin board to make the sky. Then cut out mountains from dark green, brown, and tan paper. Staple the mountains onto the blue background. Attach a piece of green paper to the bottom of the bulletin board to create the pasture. Make a pond from blue paper and a road from brown paper, and attach both to the green paper. Then, on separate sheets of paper, draw a barn, silo, fence, sun, farmhouse, and small garden. Paint them with tempera paints, cut them out, and staple them to the background paper. Make patterns for horses, cows, chickens, pigs, sheep, and ducks. Place the patterns in a learning center. Ask each child in the center to select a pattern. Have him trace around the pattern, paint the animal shape, and cut it out. Then let him attach the following material to his animal to make it look 3-D. Staple each child's animal to the bulletin board to complete the farm scene.

chicken and duck—small feathers
horse—yarn for mane and tail
pig—pink pipe cleaner for curly tail, pink button for snout
cow—thumbprints made from black tempera paint for spots, black yarn for tail
sheep—cotton balls

SNACK

Making Bread

After reading *The Little Red Hen,* have children participate in making bread. Use a boxed bread mix or the following recipe for soft pretzels:

Soft Pretzels

1 package yeast
$1\frac{1}{2}$ cups warm water
1 teaspoon salt
1 tablespoon sugar
4 cups flour
salt

Dissolve the yeast in the warm water. Add the salt, sugar, and flour. Knead the dough until smooth. Twist the dough to form letters, numbers, or shapes. Brush them with water and sprinkle them with salt. Bake at 425° for 12 to 15 minutes.

CULMINATING ACTIVITY

Barn Dance!

Read *Barn Dance!* by Bill Martin Jr. and John Archambault. Then have your children prepare for an old-fashioned classroom hoedown. Ask each child to come to school the following day dressed as a farmer. He may wear overalls, a flannel shirt, work shoes, a straw hat, a bandana, etc. As children arrive in the classroom on the day of the hoedown, have each of them construct a unique paper-plate mask of a farm animal to use with the day's activities. Then have the children sing their favorite farm songs, imitate farm animal movements, and recite farm poems. End the day by serving a snack of juice and animal crackers.

Farm Animal Cards

Use with "Counting Critters" on page 54, "Weight" and "Animal Patterning" on page 55.

Use with "Sequencing" on page 57.

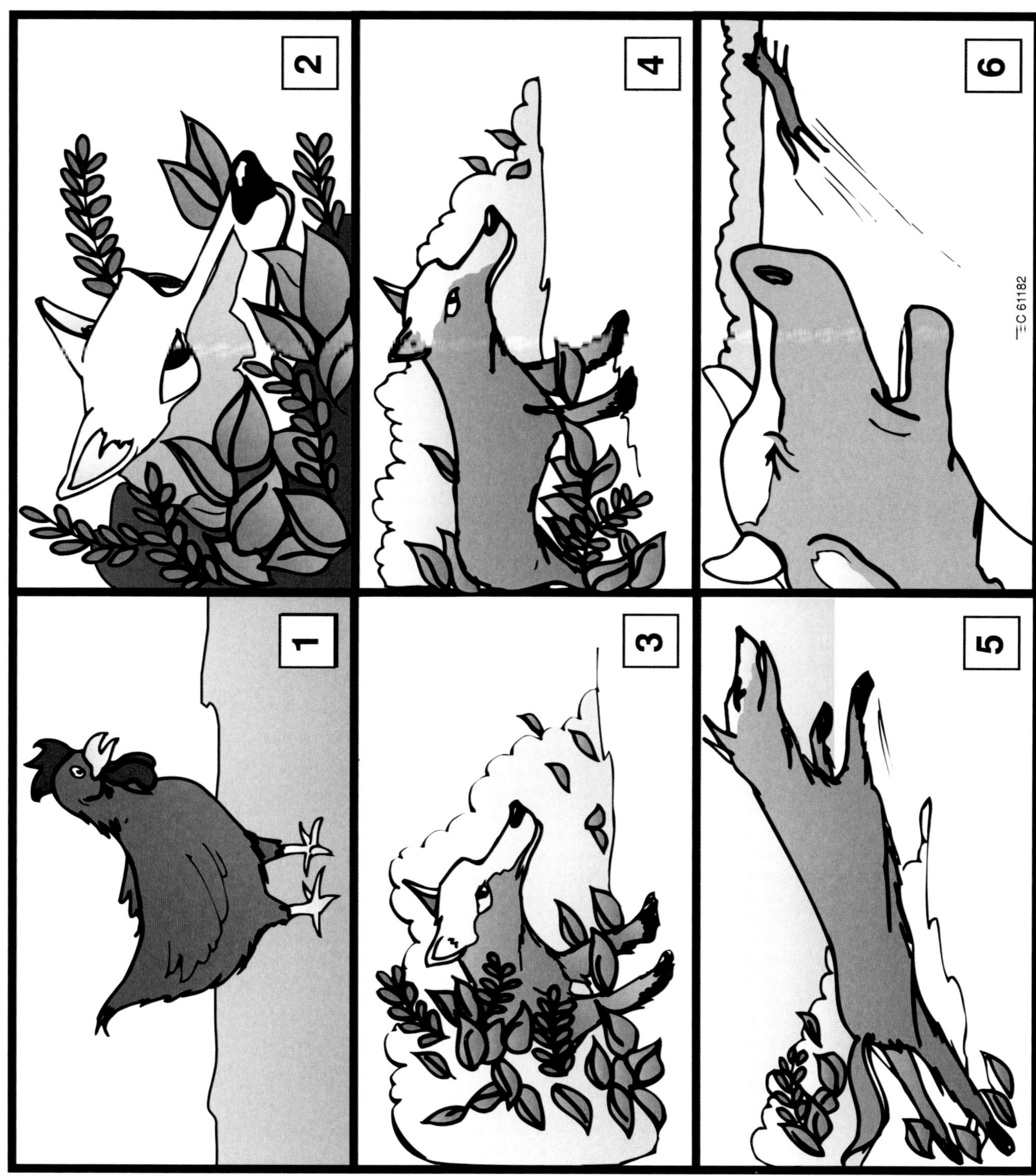

Transportation

All aboard the Transportation Express! Let your imaginations soar to destinations unknown as you travel by land, water, and air.

MATH

How We Travel

bus

car

bike

walk

Traveling To School

Draw a grid on a board or large sheet of paper. Label each row by drawing or attaching a picture of a bus, car, bike, or child walking. Have the children tell how they arrive at school and graph their responses. Discuss the results.

And They're Off!

Place several small cars and a set of wooden building blocks in a learning center. Have the children use the blocks to build a racetrack on a slick surface such as a tile floor or table. Have each child choose a car and race it with the others down the track. Ask the children to decide which car came in first, second, and third. After several races, have the children build a new track, choose a different car, and have additional races.

Types Of Transportation

Have each child bring in up to three transportation toys from home. Ask each child to put his name on his toys before bringing them to school to avoid any confusion over ownership. Place all of the toys in a box and encourage the children to think of ways to sort them into different groups such as by color, size, mode of transportation, etc. Then have your youngsters sort the vehicles. Vary the activity by asking the children to line up the toys by size from smallest to largest.

Figure It Out

Have youngsters solve word problems using the vehicles that the children brought from home for "Types Of Transportation" on page 64. Here are some examples:

1. Alan has 2 cars and 1 truck. How many vehicles does Alan have altogether? *(3)*
2. Bryan has 1 car and 2 trucks. Patrick has 2 cars and 1 truck. How many cars do the boys have altogether? *(3)* How many trucks do the boys have altogether? *(3)* How many vehicles are there in all? *(6)*
3. Brenda had 1 boat and 2 airplanes. She gave 1 airplane to Angie. How many vehicles does Brenda have now? *(2)*
4. The boys have 5 motorcycles and 5 bicycles. The girls have 5 cars and 5 helicopters. How many vehicles are there in all? *(20)*

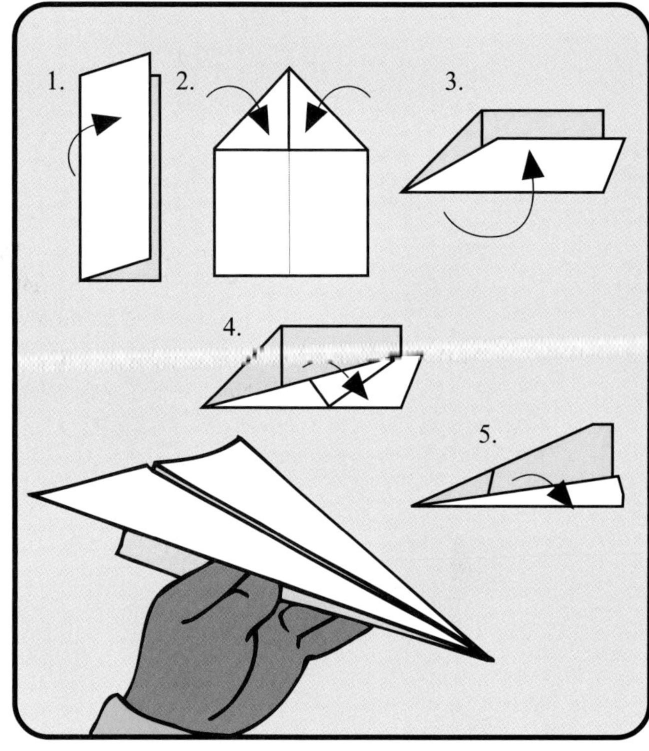

A Long Flight

Help each child use an 8 1/2" x 11" sheet of paper to make a paper airplane. Demonstrate each of the following directions, stopping after each step to check the children's work. When the airplanes are complete, have small groups of children fly their airplanes from a designated place in the classroom. Visually measure to see which plane flew the greatest distance. Then take the children outside. Have them line up, listen for a signal, and fly their airplanes. Measure the greatest distance again.

Directions for making the airplane:

1. Fold the paper in half vertically.
2. Unfold the paper and hold it vertically. Fold the top right and left corners in to the middle so they touch the crease.
3. Refold the paper so that the folded corners meet. Position the paper horizontally on the table with the fold nearest you.
4. From the point, fold one side halfway to the bottom crease.
5. Fold again, matching the edges, to the crease.
6. Turn it over and repeat steps 4 and 5 on the other side.

LANGUAGE ARTS

Following Directions

Give each child crayons and a copy of the reproducible on page 72. Read the story below. Each time a color word is read, have children trace over the appropriate dotted lines in the pictures using that color of crayon.

Sarah was so excited! She was going to Walt Disney World with her family on vacation. She picked up her red-striped suitcase and went outside. The bright yellow sun was shining. Her dad was packing the family van. The van was white with green stripes. Sarah handed the suitcase to Dad and he put it in the back of the van with the other things needed for the long trip. Suddenly the sky became dark and blue raindrops began to fall. Dad quickly packed the last of the luggage while the others got into the van.

Then the family started down the road toward the airport. In a few short minutes, Sarah saw the enormous brick building in the distance. Jets were taking off and landing on the runways nearby. Dad parked the van and got out the luggage. Sarah and the rest of her family went inside the terminal to wait. Sarah looked out the huge glass window and saw their plane. It had orange stripes on the tail and nose of the plane. It also had purple edges around the passengers' windows. Sarah could hardly wait to board the beautiful plane and begin the trip to Walt Disney World.

Cable Car Events

After reading aloud *Maybelle The Cable Car* by Virginia Lee Burton, give each child a copy of the pattern on page 73. Have her use colored pencils to draw clues about three main events on the strip as they appeared in the story. Then ask her to color the cable car and cut out the pattern and sequencing strip. Cut along the dotted lines on the cable car and insert the strip through the two slits to form a tachistoscope. Then have the child use the cable car and the strip to retell the story to a friend.

Vocabulary Word Recognition

Help the children learn the song lyrics "A Peanut Sat on a Railroad Track." Create an interactive chart by copying the song on a sheet of chart paper, omitting the following words: *peanut, track, heart, ten,* and *peanut butter.* Write each of the omitted words on a separate strip of paper. Draw a picture clue for each word on the back of the strip. Laminate the chart paper and the paper strips. Attach one-half of a Velcro circle to the back of each strip and the other half to the space on the chart where the word belongs. Have the children in a learning center use the picture clues on the backs of the strips to place the missing words in the correct spaces on the chart. Encourage each child in the group to read the poem.

Three Of A Kind

Show students a picture of a tricycle. Ask the children to look at the tricycle carefully and name each of its parts. Have the children name three parts they see that are the same. Have the children name other things that have three parts that are the same or similar: a triangle, a traffic light, *The Three Little Pigs.* List the responses on chart paper. Let each child make his own "Three Book." Cut the front and back covers and three pages in the shape of a triangle and staple them together. Have him select three things from the chart and draw one on each page of the book. Label each illustration with the corresponding words or have the child copy the words from the chart.

Alphabet Train

The children in your classroom will enjoy working together to make an alphabet train of beginning sounds. Give each child a 9" x 12" sheet of construction paper, a scrap of black paper, and a small circle tracer. Ask her to use the black paper and the circle tracer to make two wheels. Have her glue the wheels to a long strip of the construction paper to create a car for the alphabet train. Assign each child a letter and have her look through an old magazine to find a picture or pictures that begin with that letter's sound. Have her cut out the pictures and glue them to the appropriate alphabet car. Make an engine and any extra cars needed to complete the train. Mount the alphabet train on a wall in the classroom.

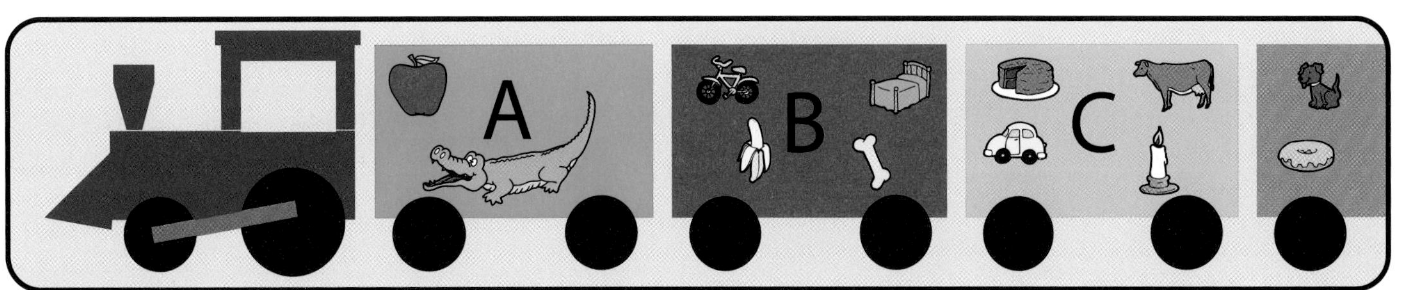

SCIENCE

Build A Vehicle

Place various building materials in a learning center, such as Legos and Flexiblocks. Have the children in the center use the materials to create different types of vehicles. Allow children to decide whether to work together to build one large vehicle or to work independently to create individual vehicles.

Wheels

Place a few wooden building blocks in a cardboard box. Have a volunteer help you with an experiment to determine the easiest way to move the box of blocks. Have the volunteer pick up the box and move it to another place in the classroom. Have him put the box on the floor and pull it to another location. Next have him push the box back to its original spot. Finally place the box in a wagon and have the child pull it across the room. Ask him which method of moving the box was the easiest. Ask him why he thought that method made moving the box easier. Have other volunteers repeat the experiment to see if they agree.

Inclined Plane

Use an inclined plane to demonstrate how different variables affect the movement of vehicles. Roll two similar cars down the inclined plane: one with wheels and one without. Discuss the advantages that wheels provide. Then race several vehicles of varying sizes and weights down the inclined plane and compare the results. Discuss how the size and weight of each vehicle affect its performance. Next change the surface of the inclined plane and compare the rate at which a vehicle travels on each surface. Suggested surfaces include thick carpet, plastic, corrugated cardboard, a bath towel, and sandpaper. Finally vary the incline of the plane before rolling a car down its surface. Discuss how the amount of incline determines the speed at which the car travels down the plane.

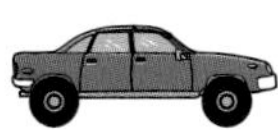

SOCIAL STUDIES

Field Trip

Organize a field trip to one of several locations to enhance children's understanding of various modes of transportation. Places might include an airport, a railroad station, or a city bus depot. When appropriate, include a tour and/or a ride on the featured mode of transportation.

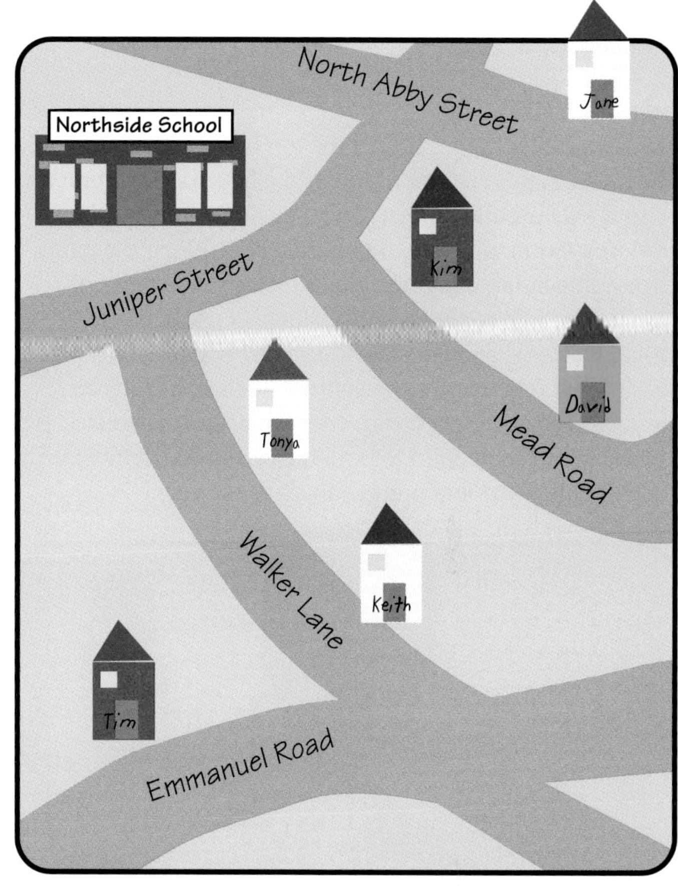

Dramatic Play

Set up a dramatic play center in the classroom where children can pretend to be riding a bus, boarding an airplane, traveling by train, or sailing on a ship. Place a props box in the center complete with a roll of tickets, a hole puncher, a memo pad, a pencil, play money, a jacket, a variety of hats, magazines, a tray of play food, luggage, and several chairs.

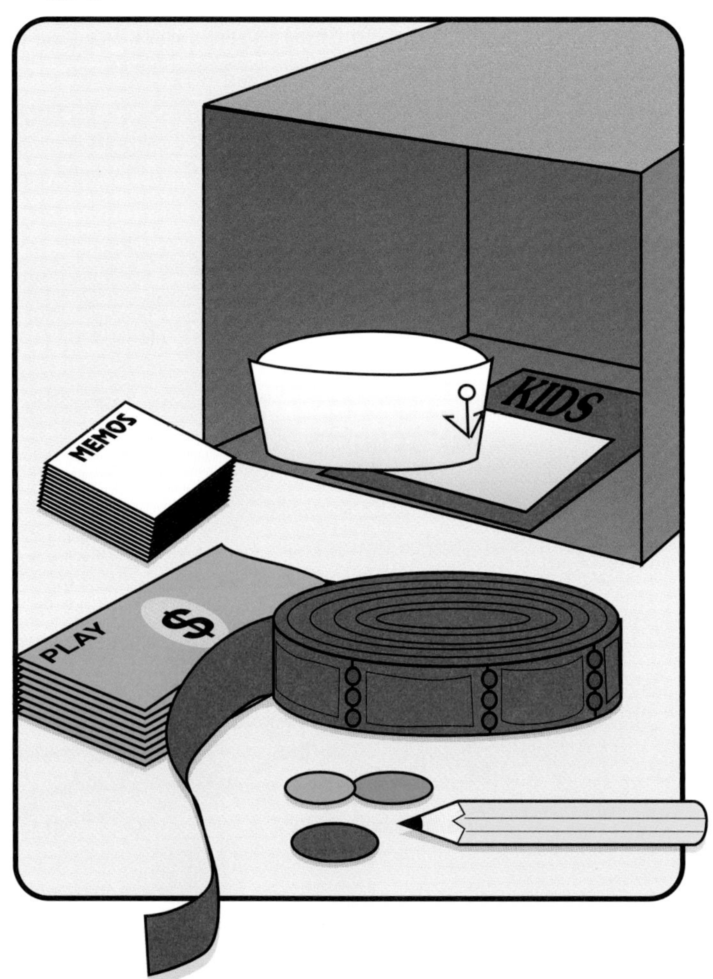

Maps

Show the children a variety of maps and point out the unique features of each one. Discuss how the people who live in the various places pictured on the maps travel from one place to another. Have the children help you create a map of how they travel to school. On a large bulletin board, construct a map of the school and the surrounding streets. Label the school and the streets. Discuss how each child travels to school. Have the children make paper buses, cars, and walking children to add to the map. Attach the graph created in "Traveling To School" on page 64 to one of the corners of or right beside the bulletin board.

ART

Box Vehicle

In advance, cut the flaps off the top of a large cardboard box. Cut a hole in the bottom of the box large enough to slip it over a child's waist. Invite students to use bright-colored tempera paints to paint the box. When the paint dries, attach large painted paper plates to the sides of the box to make wheels. Have students use scissors, glue, markers, and construction-paper scraps to make additional features for the vehicle, such as headlights, a license plate, and a horn. After the project is complete, invite each child to hold the cardboard vehicle up around his waist and pretend to drive the car.

Shape Collage

After reading several books about various types of vehicles, set up a learning center in the classroom where children can make shape collages of their favorite vehicles. Place construction paper, paper scraps, scissors, glue, and shape patterns in the center. Have each child use the paper scraps and the patterns to create his vehicle. Have him glue the vehicle on a construction-paper background and use the remaining paper scraps to make any additional features such as roads, stop signs, trees, clouds, or traffic lights. Vary the activity by having each child write a sentence about his vehicle on the collage. Bind all of the pages together with a cover to create a class book.

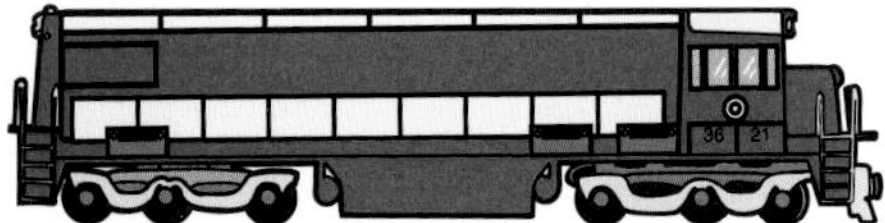

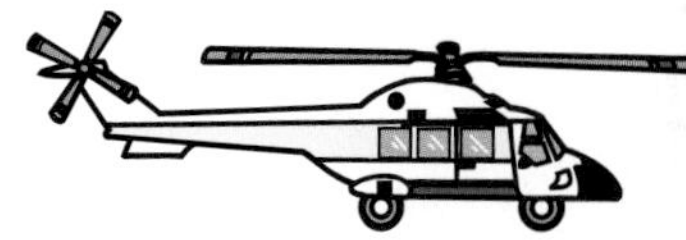

SNACK

Egg Boats

1 egg for every 2 children
mayonnaise
mustard
salt
pepper
1 slice of cheese for every 4 children
toothpicks

To create the egg boat hulls, hard-boil the eggs and peel them. Cut the eggs in half. Remove the yolks and mix them with mayonnaise, mustard, salt, and pepper. Spoon a small amount of the egg mixture into each egg half. Then cut sliced cheese into quarters to make the boat sails. Push a toothpick through each piece of cheese and insert it into the egg white.

CULMINATING ACTIVITY

Schedule a time for a vehicle parade. Have youngsters parade throughout the school pretending to ride on a train, then a plane, and so on. To add interest to the parade, let children use horns, kazoos, or other musical instruments.

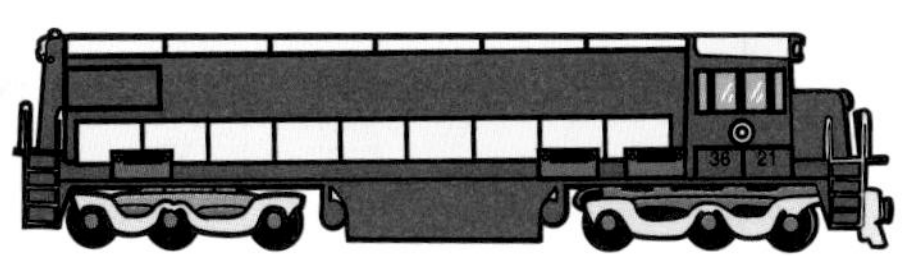

Name ____________________

Note to Teacher: Use with "Following Directions" on page 66.

Use with "Cable Car Events" on page 66.

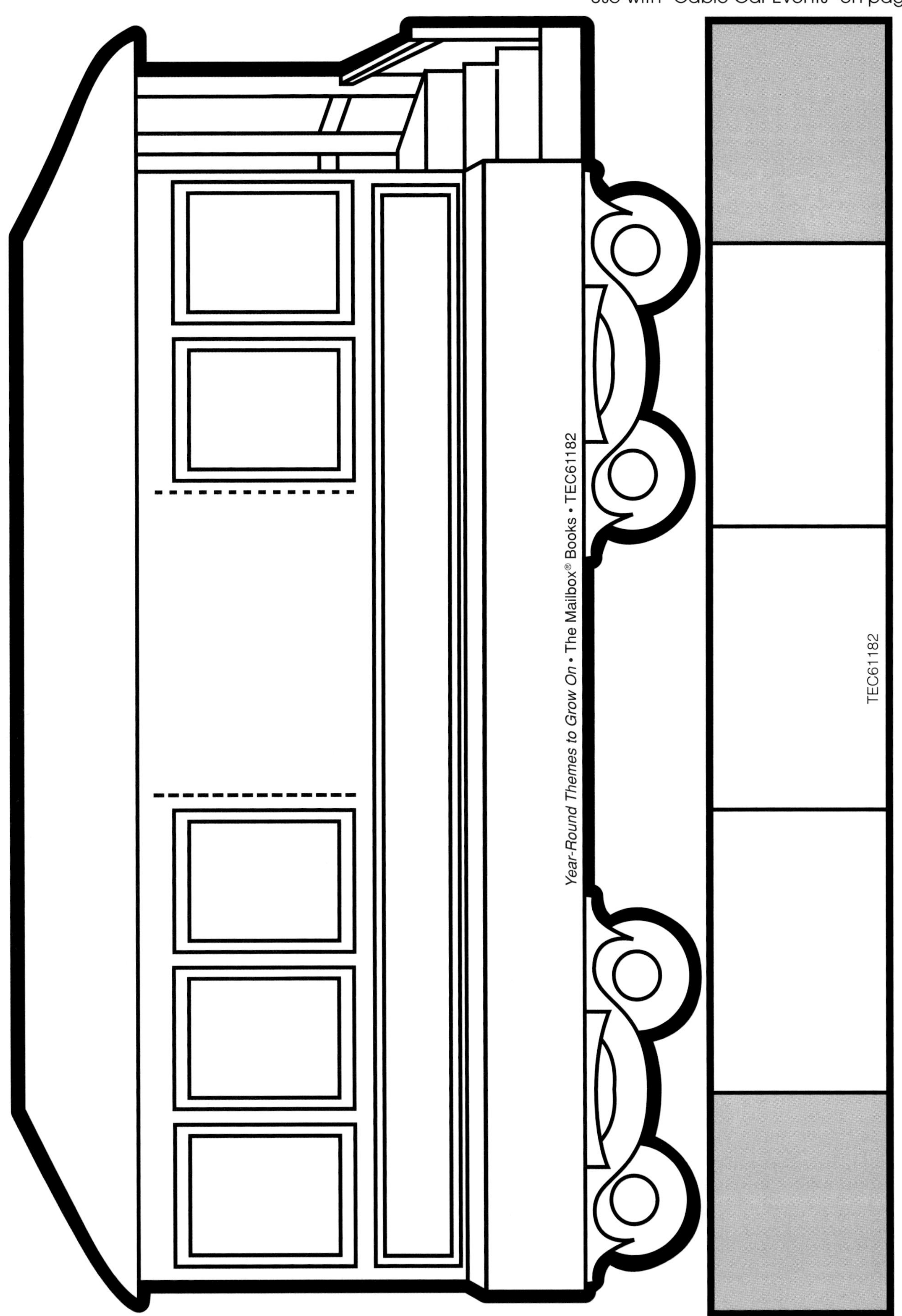

Winter Holidays

Traditions and holidays come alive during this festive winter season with ideas and activities designed to make your class more aware of cultural celebrations.

MATH

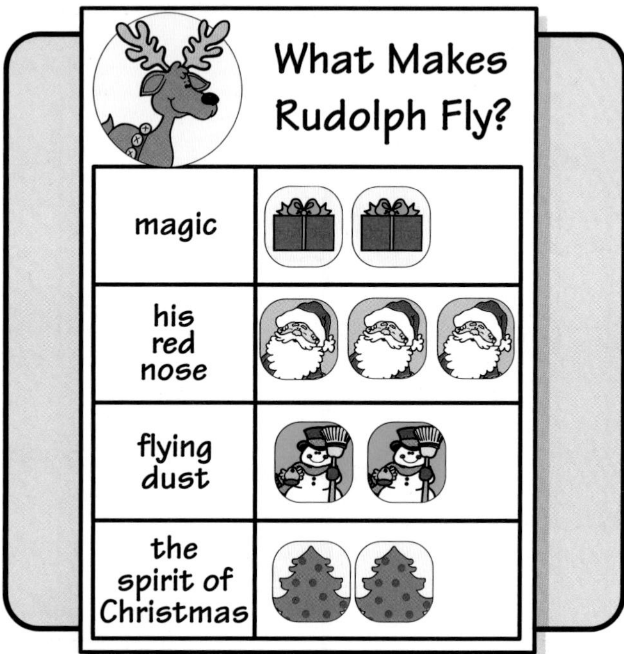

Graphing

Have each child tell you what he thinks makes Rudolph the reindeer fly. List the ideas on chart paper. Prepare a graph using four or five of the responses. Have each child place a holiday sticker beside his favorite reason. Discuss which reason received the most votes, which received the fewest votes, and why each received the votes it did.

Candy Estimation

Fill a resealable plastic bag with Christmas candy. Have each child estimate how many pieces of candy are in the bag. Write each child's name and estimate on a sheet of paper. Under close supervision, count out the candy to determine whose estimate came closest to the actual number.

Card Sorting And Counting

Have the children bring in old holiday cards. Place the cards in a large box. Have the children in a learning center classify the cards (cards with pictures of Santa, winter scenes, words only, etc.). Then have each child count the cards in each group.

Visual Memory

Collect several small, cleaned milk cartons and pairs of holiday items (candy canes, bows, ornaments, etc.). Cut the top off each carton. Wrap the bottom portion of each carton in holiday paper. Place one item under each carton. Have the children in a learning center try to locate identical items by lifting two cartons at a time. Have the children take turns and replace the cartons once they have looked under them. A child who finds two matching objects may keep them until the game ends. Replace the items under the cartons with two new matching items.

Countdown Santa

Duplicate the counting grid (page 82) on red construction paper for each child. Duplicate the Santa hat pattern on page 83 to make cardboard patterns for tracers. Have each child trace Santa's hat on red construction paper and Santa's head on pink construction paper. Help each child cut out the hat and head. Have him use paper scraps to make a nose and two eyes. Help him cut out the counting grid and glue it to the head at the dotted line. Have him glue the eyes, nose, and hat to the head. Glue cotton balls to the hat to create fur and to the head to make Santa's hair and mustache. Each child can take his Santa home along with a parent letter (see below) and glue a cotton ball on the counting grid each of the 24 days before Santa arrives.

Reindeer Story Problems

Have the children listen carefully to each reindeer story problem. Then use reindeer cutouts to help youngsters find the answer to each problem.

Once there were three reindeer getting ready to pull a sleigh. They started to pull, but the sleigh was too heavy. Three more reindeer came to help. How many reindeer in all were pulling the sleigh? *(6)*

Dasher, Dancer, Prancer, and Vixen were getting ready for Christmas Eve. Comet, Cupid, Donner, and Blitzen joined them. How many reindeer in all were getting ready for Christmas Eve? *(8)*

Santa took eight of his reindeer for a practice flight. Four of them became sick and had to stop. How many reindeer were left to fly with Santa? *(4)*

It was the day after Christmas. Dasher, Dancer, Prancer, Vixen, Comet, Cupid, Donner, Blitzen, and Rudolph were getting ready for a nap. Mrs. Claus gave each of them a snack. Four of the reindeer went to sleep. How many of the reindeer were still awake? *(5)*

Santa's elves need to put bells on the reindeer for the Christmas Eve journey. They found four reindeer in the stable and three on the roof. How many reindeer did the elves find? *(7)*

LANGUAGE ARTS

Festive Writing

Help each child in a learning center make a holiday book he can write and read independently. Write several holiday words (such as *bow, candle, tree, star, bell, stocking,* etc.) on individual cards. Illustrate each word by drawing or gluing a picture on each card. Print the sentence, "I like a ________________," at the bottom of a sheet of paper. Duplicate a quantity of this sheet to make pages for each book. Print the title "Things I Like During The Holidays" on the front of large sheets of folded construction paper. Place the cards, book pages, book covers, crayons, and pencils in a learning center. Have each child in the center choose a card and copy the word in the blank on a book page. Have her draw a picture of that object above the sentence. Have her complete several pages. Staple them inside a cover to make an individual holiday book.

Holiday Letter Boxes

Remove the tops from five large gift boxes. Cover the boxes with holiday wrapping paper. Attach an alphabet letter to the side of each box using tape or Velcro so the letter can be easily changed. Collect several small items from the classroom that begin with the letters that are on the five boxes. Place the items in a large holiday shopping bag. Have the children take each object from the shopping bag and place it in the box labeled with the letter that has the beginning corresponding sound.

Letter Recognition

Draw the outline of a large Christmas tree on a board. Draw several circles on the tree to represent ornaments. Write a letter in each circle. Have each child in a small group name a letter. If she names the letter correctly, she may erase the letter and the circle. The game ends when all of the circles have been erased. Vary the activity using numerals in the circles.

Brainstorming

Read and discuss *Alexander And The Wind-Up Mouse* by Leo Lionni. Then ask the class to describe what Annie, the owner of the wind-up mouse, planned to do with her unwanted toys after her birthday party. Next have the children think of other ways Annie could have disposed of her toys (sold them at a yard sale, donated them to a charity, given them to a needy child, etc.). Finally place a box for unwanted toys in the classroom. Tell the children they may bring unwanted toys from home and place them in the box. Then take the box of toys to Goodwill or another charitable organization.

Needs And Wants

Read the book *Claude The Dog: A Christmas Story* by Dick Gackenbach. Discuss how Claude demonstrated generosity and compassion by giving all of his holiday gifts to a homeless dog. Discuss the differences between needs and wants. Help the children make a list of things that they need and a list of things they want. Explain to your children that homeless children do not have many of the things they need or want. Ask the children if they would like to help a needy child. Send a note home and ask parents to send in small, inexpensive items (toothbrush, socks, mittens, crayons, hats) that could be donated. Decorate a large box and place it in the room. Have the children place their donated items in the box. Arrange to take the items to a shelter or an agency that helps the needy.

SOCIAL STUDIES

Saving Money

Later in the week, review the lesson on *wants* and *needs.* Have the children think of things they would like to save their money to buy. Make a list of the items on a sheet of chart paper. Place this list beside the lists of needs and wants in a learning center. Give each child three sheets of paper and help her label them "Needs," "Wants," and "Save For." Have her draw something she needs on the first page, something she wants on the second page, and something she would like to save for on the last page. Bind the pages together to create an individual book.

Edible Christmas Candles

Follow the directions and have the children assemble an edible fruit candle.

Fruit Candle

1 pineapple ring
½ banana
1 cherry
1 toothpick
1 small paper plate

Place the pineapple ring on a small paper plate. Set the half of a banana in the hole of the pineapple. Insert a toothpick in the cherry and push the other end through the top of the banana.

Hanukkah

Hanukkah is a Jewish festival that lasts for eight days and is based on an ancient event. Judah Maccabee led the Jewish people in a victory over the Syrians. The Jewish people wanted to celebrate by lighting a lamp to rededicate the temple. However, the people could find only enough oil to burn the lamp for one day. Amazingly, the oil lasted for eight days.

The *menorah* is a candlestick that holds nine candles. Eight candles represent the eight days that the lamp burned. The *shammash* or "helper" candle is used to light the other candles. Each night of Hanukkah, Jewish families gather to light a candle on the menorah and share special foods, songs, games, and gifts. *Latkes,* potato pancakes served at least once during Hanukkah, can be made using this recipe.

Latkes

2 cups grated potatoes
1 small onion
1 teaspoon salt
¼ teaspoon pepper
1 tablespoon flour
½ teaspoon baking powder
2 eggs, well-beaten
Oil
Applesauce

Peel the potatoes and soak them in cold water. Drain the potatoes and grate. Grate the onion and mix it with the potatoes. Add salt and pepper. Mix in the flour and baking powder. Add the eggs. Drop the mixture by teaspoons into a hot, well-greased frying pan. Flatten latkes with the back of a spoon. Brown both sides. Drain on paper towels. Serve latkes with applesauce.

Las Posadas

Mexican-Americans celebrate Las Posadas during the Christmas season. Each night from December 16 to December 24, friends and neighbors gather to form a parade and act out Mary and Joseph's search for a *posada,* or inn. Two children assume the roles of Mary and Joseph and lead the parade from house to house. On the final night, the parade reaches a designated destination and a tiny figure of Baby Jesus is placed in a manger scene. In south-central Texas some cities line the streets with luminarias during the Las Posadas celebration. Have each child make a luminaria to take home for the holidays. Give each child a white paper sack. Have him decorate the bag and fill it with one to two inches of sand. If desired, parents can push a tea candle into the center of the sand.

Kwanzaa

Kwanzaa is a holiday observed by some African-Americans in celebration of the African harvest. It is also a time for African-Americans to honor their ancestors and celebrate the joys of family. Kwanzaa begins on December 26 and ends on January 1. On each of the seven days, families gather to light a candle, discuss one of the seven principles of African-American culture, and exchange homemade gifts. To help the children understand Kwanzaa's focus on the harvest, have each child bring a fruit or vegetable from home. Place the food in a decorated box and donate the food box to a needy family.

SCIENCE

Evergreen Trees

Arrange a time with the local forestry department for a representative to come to your class and talk about the characteristics of evergreen trees. Take the class on a nature walk around the school grounds to look for evergreens.

ART

Gift Tags

Collect old holiday cards. Cut the back off each one and use a hole puncher to punch holes around the outside edges of the cards. Have each child in a small group choose one of the cards and use a piece of yarn to lace around it. Secure the ends of the yarn by tying them together. Help each child address the card, wrap her cinnamon ornament (see page 81) or other gift in tissue paper, and place it in a white paper bag. Fold the top of the bag down, punch two holes in the top, and lace a piece of yarn through the two holes. Tie the gift tag to the bag.

Bulletin Board

After reading aloud *The Polar Express* by Chris Van Allsburg, have the children create a magical train ride across a large bulletin board in the classroom. Cover the top half of the board with light blue paper. Cover the bottom with white. Use construction paper to make a railroad track that winds its way through the snow. Have a group of children make houses, shops, trees, and small animals from scraps of brightly colored construction paper. Staple these around the railroad tracks. Have another group make a train. Give the children construction paper and several shape patterns. Have them trace the shapes, cut them out, and assemble them to make a engine and several boxcars. Staple the train to the track. Add cotton snow to the tops of the buildings and star stickers to the sky.

Gingerbread Houses

Collect a small milk carton for each child in the classroom. Rinse the inside of each carton, let it dry, and staple the top closed. Have each child paint his milk carton and then glue on pom-poms, craft foam shapes, and sequins so it resembles a gingerbread house.

SNACK

Holiday Cider

1 gallon apple cider or apple juice
1 cinnamon stick per child

Pour the cider into a saucepan. Heat the cider. Pour it into individual cups, allow to cool slightly, and serve each cup with a cinnamon stick. This makes approximately 24 servings.

CULMINATING ACTIVITY

Cinnamon Ornaments

Make ornaments using cinnamon and applesauce and fill your classroom with the wonderful smell of the holiday season.

To make 12 small ornaments use
- $3\frac{3}{4}$ oz. ground cinnamon
- $\frac{1}{2}$ cup applesauce

Mix the cinnamon and applesauce until the mixture is the consistency of cookie dough. Roll the dough between two sheets of waxed paper. Have each child use a small cookie cutter to cut out an ornament. Use a drinking straw to punch a hole in the top of each ornament. Allow ornaments to dry about 36 hours, turning them occasionally. Thread a piece of ribbon through the hole in each ornament and tie it to make a hanger. The ornaments may be given to family members or friends.

Santa's Beard/Counting Grid

Use with "Countdown Santa" on page 75.

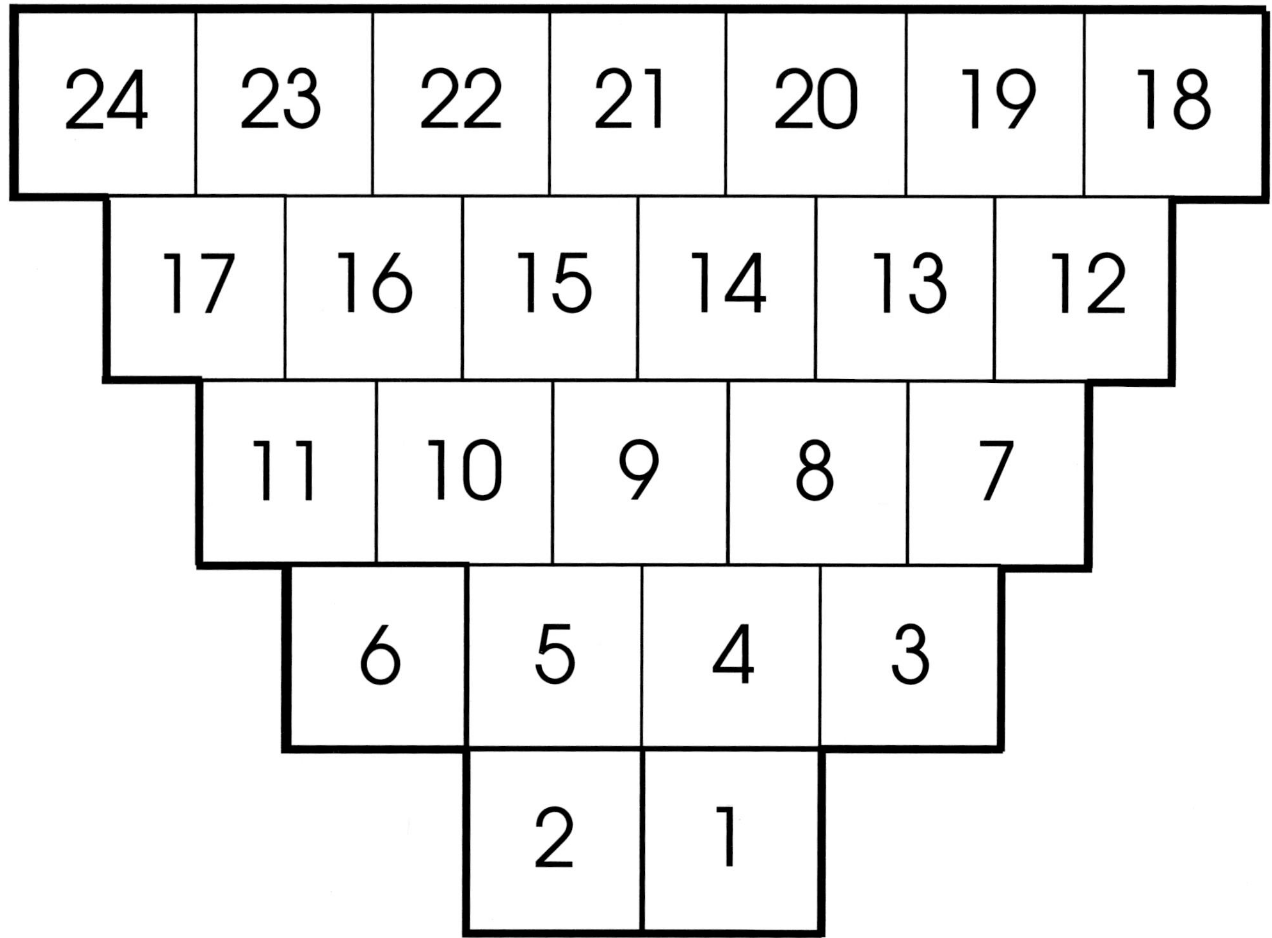

Santa Patterns

Use with "Countdown Santa" on page 75.

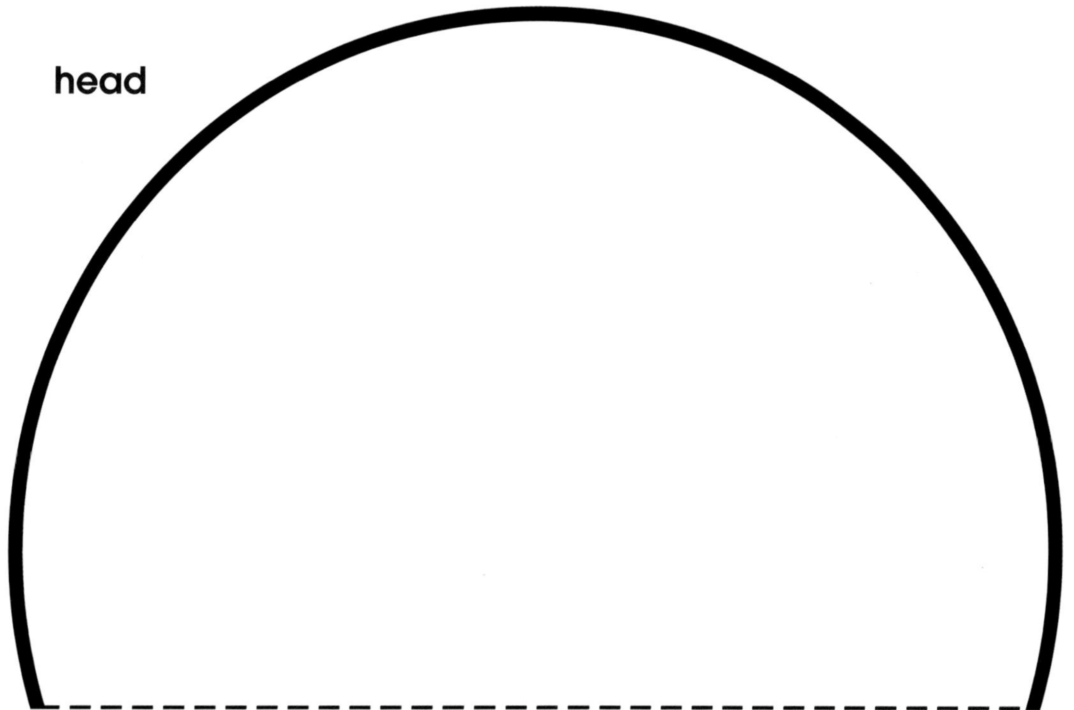

Glue the counting grid here.

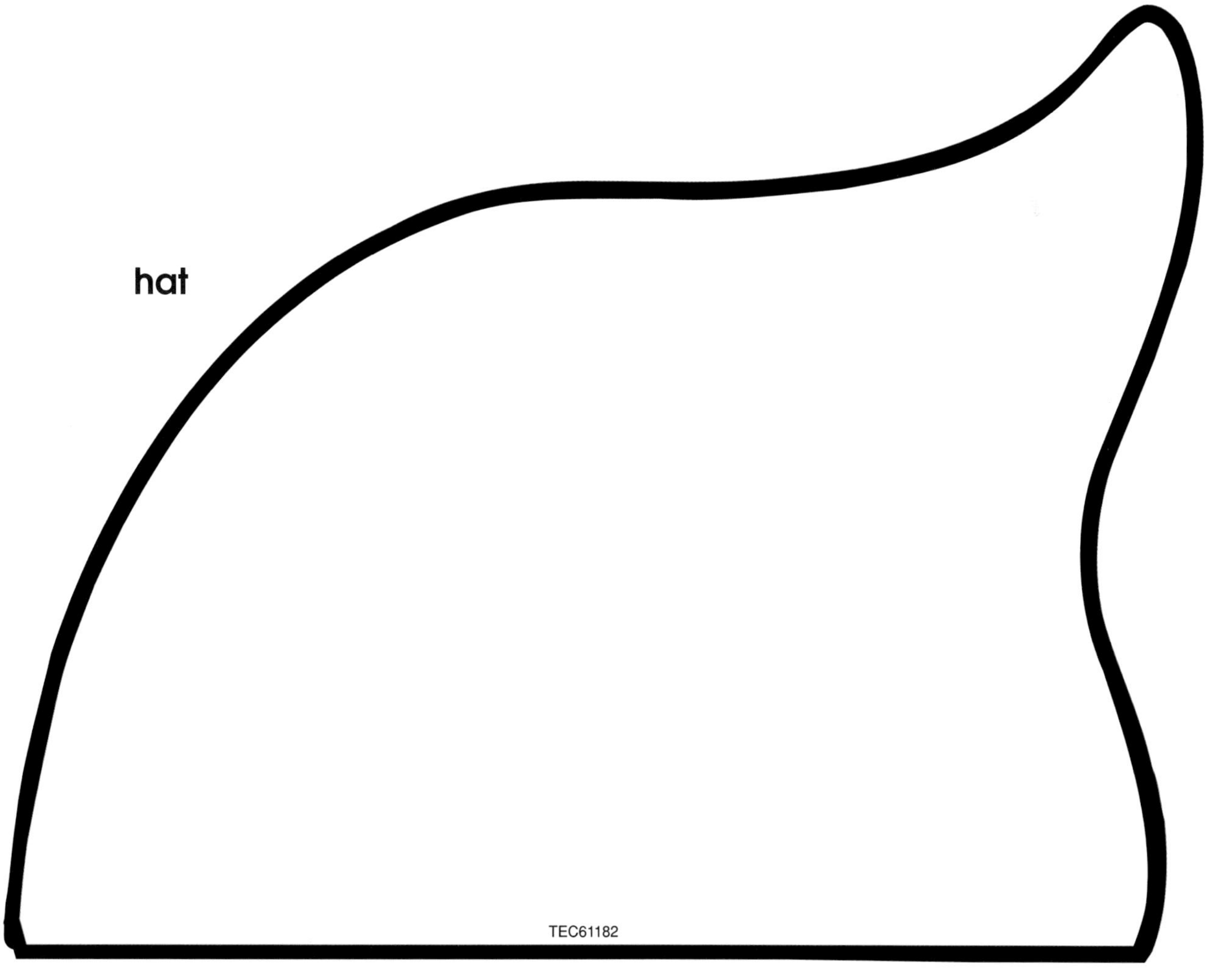

hat

TEC61182

Fairy Tales

Your children will live happily ever after in the enchanted land of fairy tales and fantasy. This focus on make-believe will involve your youngsters in many enjoyable hands-on experiences.

MATH

Let Down Your Hair

How long was Rapunzel's hair? Let the children in your class discover the answer to this question while practicing estimation and measuring skills. To prepare for the activity, braid several long strands of yarn to resemble a ponytail. Secure the ends with ribbon. Show the ponytail to your children. Ask them to pretend that it is Rapunzel's hair. Then, using a nonstandard unit of measurement, have each child estimate its length. For example, it is 5 pencils long or 30 Duplo blocks long. Record each child's estimation on a sheet of paper. Then have your students sit in a circle. Lay the braid on the floor and measure it. Write the actual measurement on the board and have your children compare their estimations to see which child was the closest.

What's In A Name?

There are 15 letters in the name *Rumpelstiltskin.* Write the name on the board and then count the letters. Next, have each child write her first name on a sheet of paper. Tell her to count the letters in her name. Have the children decide whose names have the most letters, the fewest letters, and the same number of letters. Then place their names in descending order under the name *Rumpelstiltskin.* To vary the activity, help each child write her last name on her paper. Have each child decide which of her names has more letters.

Sizing Up Teddies

After reading *Goldilocks And The Three Bears,* discuss size relationships (small, medium, and large) with your youngsters. Then have your students bring in teddy bears from home. Allow students to line up the teddy bears starting with the smallest and going to the biggest bear.

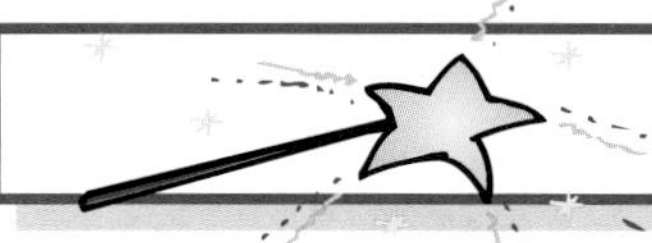

If The Shoe Fits

Read the story *Cinderella* to your class. Then ask your youngsters to describe the characteristic that made Cinderella's shoes special. Afterward let the children participate in a sorting activity and compare shoes. Place a hoop on the floor. Ask each child to put her shoe inside it (teacher, too). Lay a second hoop beside the first. Have a student volunteer sort the shoes into two groups using an attribute such as *tie/no tie, color,* or *the size of the heel.* Then ask the remaining members of the class to decide which attribute was used for sorting. Repeat the activity several times with other student volunteers.

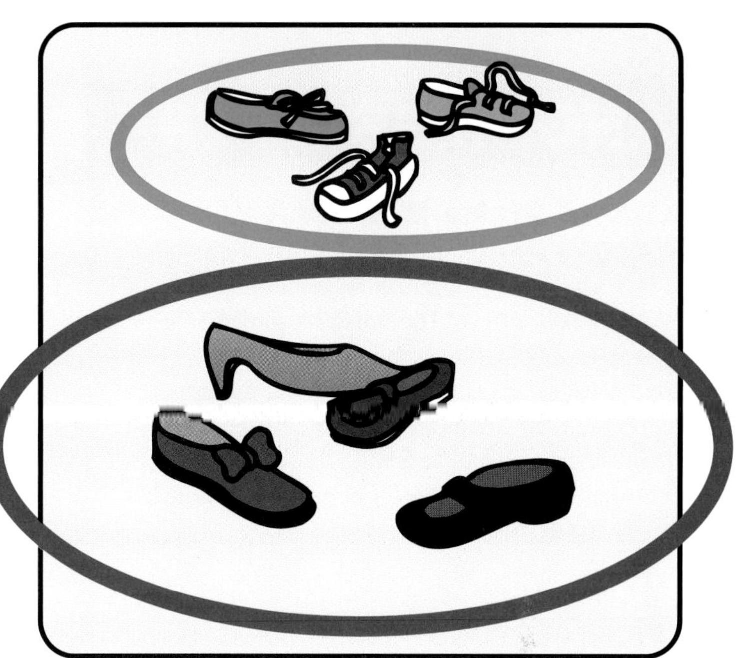

One Hundred Kisses

The wolf is the villain in *Little Red Riding Hood* and *The Three Little Pigs.* However, in *The Wolf's Chicken Stew* by Keiko Kasza, the wolf has a change of heart and receives one hundred kisses from a family of baby chicks. Read this delightful story to your children. Then place several containers of small objects such as pom-poms or candy kisses in a learning center. Have your students help each other count one hundred items from each of the containers.

The Seven Dwarfs

The seven dwarfs from the Walt Disney version of *Snow White* can be easily recognized by children. Obtain a picture of each dwarf from a coloring book or poster. Glue each picture to a separate square of tagboard for durability. Teach the dwarfs' names to your children. Then place the pictures in a row and ask the children to name the dwarf that is third, fifth, second, etc. Then change the order of the pictures and repeat the activity. Next have each child decide which dwarf is his favorite. Place the pictures in a row on the floor. Then give each child a block and ask him to place it above the picture of his favorite dwarf. Count the number of blocks in each stack to determine which dwarf is the class favorite.

Run, Run, As Fast As You Can

After reading *The Gingerbread Boy,* give each child a copy of the reproducible on page 92. Help him connect the dots to create his own Gingerbread Boy.

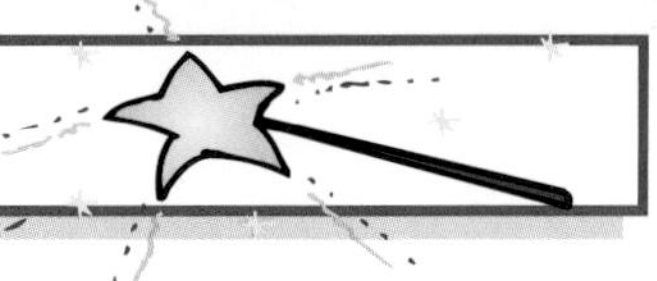

LANGUAGE ARTS

Real And Make-Believe

There are many aspects of fairy tales that are imaginary. Talk about the differences in something real and something make-believe. Then discuss some of the make-believe people, places, and things in various fairy tales. Next ask your youngsters to cut out pictures of real and imaginary things from old magazines. Attach two large sheets of paper to a wall. Label one "Real" and the other "Make-Believe." Let each child glue his pictures to the corresponding paper.

Character Hunt

Select two characters from each of several fairy tales. Write the name of each character on separate index cards. Also, paste a picture of the character on the card. Give each child a card and have him read the name of the character. Then ask him to walk around the room and find the classmate with the name of another character from the same fairy tale. Tell the pairs to sit together on the floor until everyone has found his partner.

ABC Beanstalk

Make a giant beanstalk from strips of green construction paper. Then use a leaf pattern to make twenty-six green leaves. Write an uppercase letter on the front of each leaf and a lowercase letter on the back. Place the beanstalk on the floor in the classroom. Let a small group of children work together to arrange the uppercase and then the lowercase letters in alphabetical order. Provide students with an alphabet strip to use as a guide.

Compare And Contrast

Read the traditional versions of *Little Red Riding Hood, Goldilocks And The Three Bears,* and *The Three Little Pigs* aloud to your children. Then read *Lon Po Po: A Red-Riding Hood Story From China* translated by Ed Young, *Deep In The Forest* by Brinton Turkle, and *The True Story Of The 3 Little Pigs!* by A. Wolf as told to Jon Scieszka. Compare and contrast these new versions with the familiar tales by making a list of how the pairs are the same and another list of how they are different. Then place a copy of each fairy tale on a table in the classroom. Let each child indicate the version she liked best by placing a teddy bear counter beside the book.

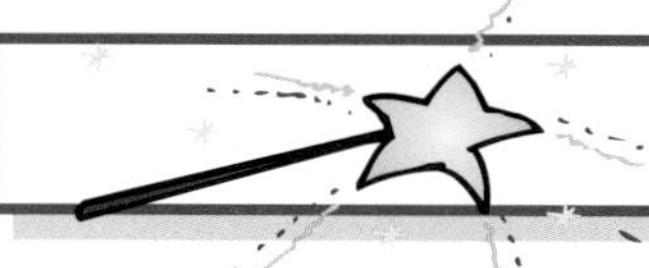

Finger-Nose Puppets

Make several copies of the reproducible on page 93 on white construction paper. Give a copy to each child in a small group. Have him color the puppets and then help him cut them out. To hold a puppet, have him put his index finger through the hole. Then let him use the puppets to tell the story of *Goldilocks And The Three Bears.*

Happily Ever After

Read *The Frog Prince* to your children. Then talk about what happened to the prince and princess after they were married. Next read *The Frog Prince, Continued* by Jon Scieszka. Discuss how the writer continued the fairy tale. Then brainstorm several ideas for continuing another fairy tale such as *Sleeping Beauty* or *The Elves And The Shoemaker.* Choose one of the ideas and help your children develop a story line. Print the story on chart paper as it is dictated by the children. Then assign each child part of the story to copy and illustrate. Bind the pages together to create a class book.

Who Am I?

After reading aloud several fairy tales, ask your children simple questions such as those listed below.

I slept for one hundred years after pricking my finger on a spindle. Who am I? *(Sleeping Beauty)*

I was locked up in a tall tower by an old witch. Who am I? *(Rapunzel)*

I traded my cow, Milky White, for magic beans. Who am I? *(Jack)*

I was placed in a glass coffin after eating a poisoned apple. Who am I? *(Snow White)*

I retrieved a golden ball from a fountain for a princess. Who am I? *(The Frog Prince)*

I spun straw into gold for the miller's daughter. Who am I? *(Rumpelstiltskin)*

I took food to my sick grandmother. Who am I? *(Red Riding Hood)*

I changed a pumpkin into a beautiful carriage. Who am I? *(Cinderella's fairy godmother)*

Teeny-Tiny Theater

Collect small toys, puppets, or cutouts that resemble the characters from several fairy tales. Place each set of items in a separate container with a lid. Label each container with the name of the fairy tale. For example, for *Goldilocks And The Three Bears,* place three toy bears and a doll with blond hair in an empty coffee can or oatmeal box. Then use the toys in a container to tell a story. Ask a child to describe the order in which the characters appeared in the story. Let the child take the items out of the container as he describes the sequence. Display the container in a learning center. Let the children in the center use it to tell the story to each other. Repeat the activity with another container of story props.

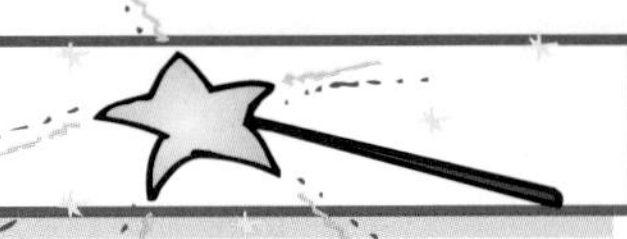

SCIENCE

Mysterious Water

Fairy tales have many mystical elements. Your students will enjoy this fun-filled activity while making colorful water. For each child in a small group, place one tablespoon of water in a bowl. Add three drops of food coloring and mix well. Then fill a plastic jar with mineral oil. Use an eyedropper to add two or three drops of colored water to the oil. Secure the lid tightly. Then tip the jar in different directions and watch the mysterious colored water float.

Hocus-Pocus

Tell your children you have a paper towel that can stay dry in water! Crumple a paper towel into a ball and place it in the bottom of a glass. Push the glass, open end first, straight down into a container of water. (Make sure the glass does not tilt.) Then lift the glass out of the water and remove the paper towel. Tell your children the paper towel stayed dry because the air in the glass did not let the water touch it. Return the paper-towel ball to the glass and insert the glass into the water again. This time tilt the glass so air bubbles can escape. Lift the glass out of the water, remove the paper towel from the glass, and have youngsters feel the wet towel.

Abracadabra

Here's another fun activity to stir up interest in your class. Give each child in a small group two sugar cubes, two stirring sticks, a cup of warm water, and a cup of cold water. Tell the children they will watch a race between warm water and cold water to see which one can melt a sugar cube first. Before the race begins, let each child predict the winner. Then give a signal and ask each child to place one sugar cube in the cup of warm water and one in the cup of cold water. Have him stir both cups of water with the stirring sticks until one of the cubes dissolves completely. Discuss the results of the race. Ask the children to tell why one sugar cube dissolved faster than the other.

What Big Eyes You Have!

When Little Red Riding Hood saw the wolf lying in her grandmother's bed, she was surprised at her large ears, eyes, and teeth. Each child will enjoy making small objects look bigger with this simple activity. Cut the bottom out of an oatmeal box. Then cut two openings in the box near the bottom as shown. Place a piece of plastic wrap loosely over the top of the box. Secure the plastic wrap with a rubber band. Press the center of the plastic wrap in slightly to form a bowl. Fill the bowl with water. Then slide a small object through an opening so it is inside the oatmeal box, and look at it through the water. The object will be magnified.

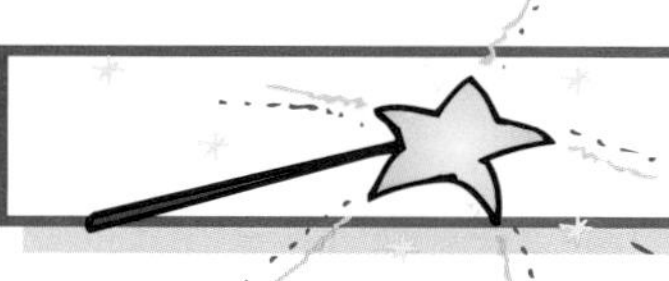

SOCIAL STUDIES

Stranger Danger

Red Riding Hood was almost eaten by a strange wolf on her way to Grandma's house. Hansel was locked in a cage and Gretel had to work for a witch because the pair stopped at a strange house in the woods. Use these two characters to illustrate how important it is not to talk to strangers or accept gifts from them. Then invite a representative from your local police department to present a program on stranger danger.

Secret Pal

In the story *The Elves And The Shoemaker,* a pair of elves secretly helps a poor shoemaker and his wife. Read the story to your children. Then talk about what it means to be a secret pal. Ask your class if they would like to be a secret pal to another class for one week. Ask your children to suggest things they could do secretly for the other class. Each day, leave something made by your children outside the other class's door. On the last day of the activity, let your youngsters reveal their identity to their secret pals.

Manners Party

When Goldilocks visited the home of the Three Bears, she did not use good manners. She entered the house without being invited, ate their food without asking, broke a chair, and made a mess in every room. Discuss how Goldilocks should have behaved. Then ask the children to pretend they have been invited to the Three Bears' house for a manners party. Talk about how children should act at the party. Help them make a list of manners, similar to those listed below, on a sheet of chart paper. Then show each child how to prepare her place setting correctly using a plate, a cup, plastic utensils, and a napkin. Place baskets of snack foods on each table and let the party begin!

Manners To Remember

Place a napkin in your lap before eating.
Use the napkin to wipe your face and hands.
Do not reach for food. Ask that it be passed to you.
Use the words *please* and *thank you.*
Do not talk with food in your mouth.

ART

Magic Wand

Each child in a small group can create a magic wand with a few materials and a little imagination. Give each child a cardboard tube approximately twelve inches in length. Have him paint the tube with bright-colored paint; then trace a star pattern on construction paper and cut it out. Invite him to decorate the star with markers, stickers, or glitter; then flatten one end of the cardboard tube and staple the star to it. Complete the wand by attaching crepe-paper streamers or ribbon to the tube at the base of the star.

Weaving

Fairy tales such as *Rumpelstiltskin* and *The Emperor's New Clothes* include characters who can weave. Show your children how they too can become weavers with this simple activity. Cut several circles from heavy cardboard. Draw a circle in the center of each cardboard circle. Then draw eight lines that extend from the center circle to the edge of the cardboard. Cut along each of the straight lines using an X-acto knife. Give each child in a small group one of these cardboard circles. Let him paint the center with bright-colored paint. Allow the paint to dry. Secure a piece of yarn to the back of the circle with tape. Ask him to weave the yarn on the cardboard circle by pulling the yarn through the cuts in an over-and-under fashion. Secure the end of the yarn to the back of the circle when the weaving is complete.

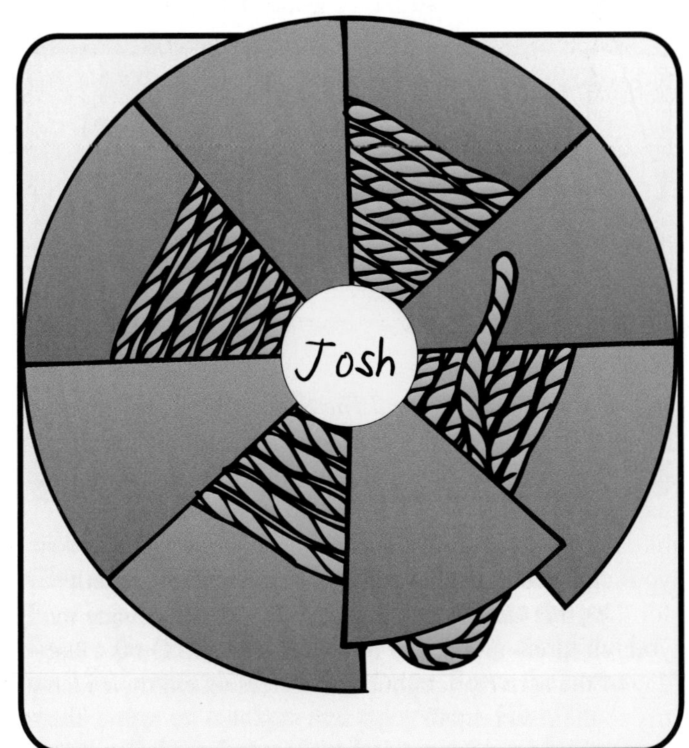

SNACK

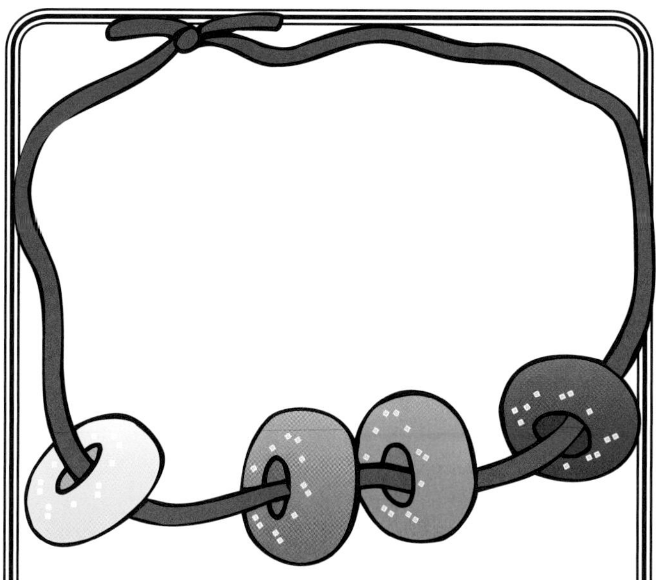

Candy Jewels

Once the old witch was gone, Hansel and Gretel filled their pockets with her gold, silver, and precious jewels. Let each child in a small group make a bracelet representative of the witch's jewelry. Have her string four or five Fruit Loops on a licorice string. Then tie it around her wrist.

CULMINATING ACTIVITY

Character Day

On the last day of the unit, ask each child to pretend to be his favorite fairy-tale character. Have the remaining students guess which character each child is.

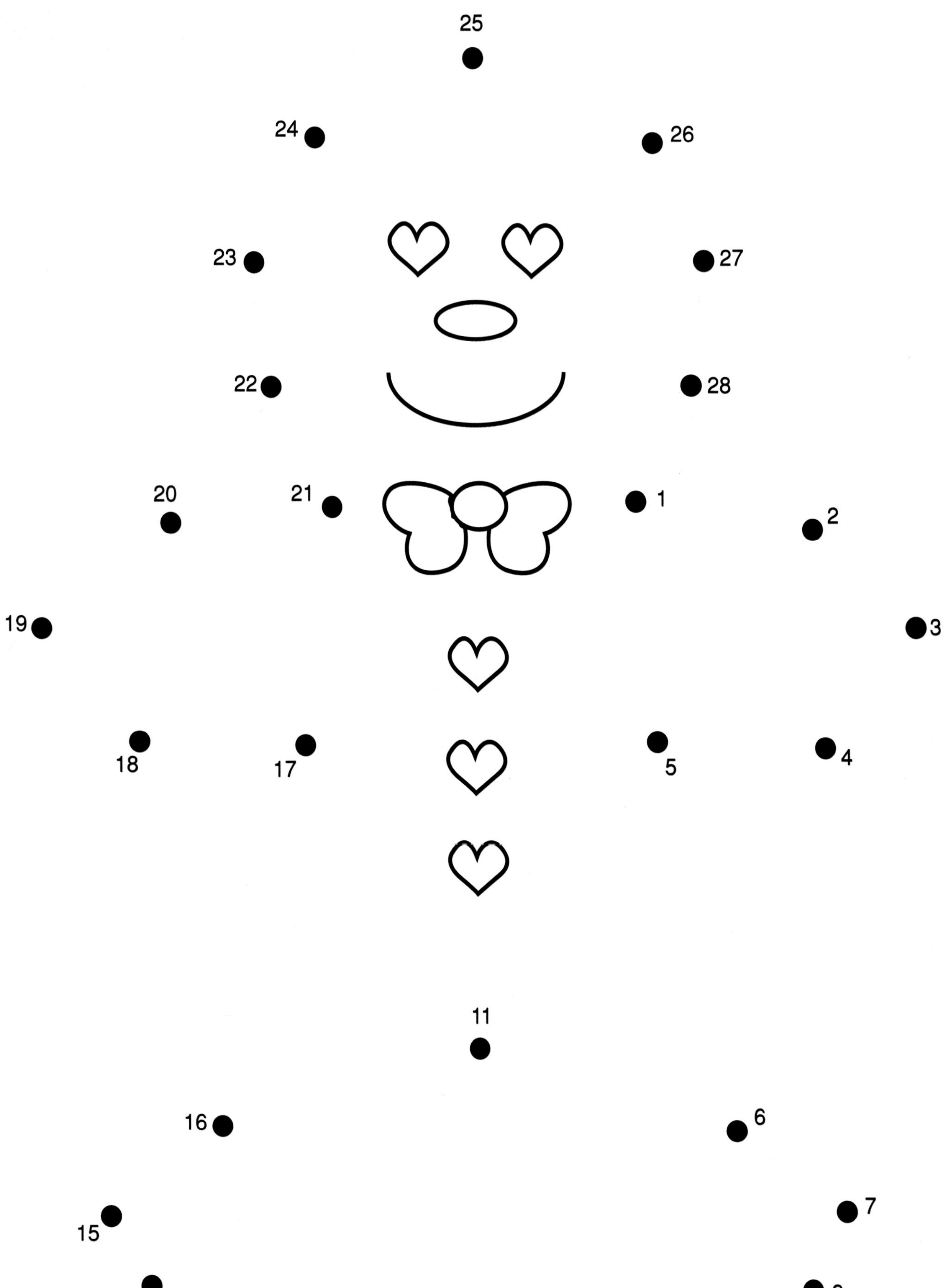

 Note to the teacher: Use with "Run, Run as Fast As You Can" on page 85.

Fairy Tale Puppets

Use with "Finger-Nose Puppets" on page 87.

Dinosaurs

Present a learning playground of the prehistoric world of dinosaurs where children enhance their skills and creativity through hands-on activities.

MATH

Dinosaur Classification

Give a small group of children a variety of small plastic dinosaurs. Have the children sort and categorize the dinosaurs by color, kind, or size.

Digging Up Dinosaurs

Bury several plastic dinosaurs in a sand table. Give each child in a small group an empty container. Have the children dig in the sand, find the dinosaurs, and place them in the containers. At the conclusion of the activity, have each child total the number of dinosaurs he found.

Favorite Dinosaurs

Triceratops

Apatosaurus

Stegosaurus

Tyrannosaurus Rex

Graphing Dinosaurs

Draw a large grid on the board or a large piece of paper. Draw or attach different dinosaur pictures to the left-hand side of the grid. Have each child vote for his favorite dinosaur. Graph the responses by coloring in the squares on the grid.

Tyrannosaurus

Give each child a copy of the tyrannosaurus reproducible puzzle on page 102. Have her color the dinosaur and cut it apart on the dotted lines. Have her find the dinosaur's front, middle, and end and place them in the correct order on a piece of construction paper. Have her glue the three pieces to the construction paper.

Dinosaur Patterning

Have the children in a small group create original dinosaur patterns using scrap paper, stamp pads, and several rubber dinosaur stamps.

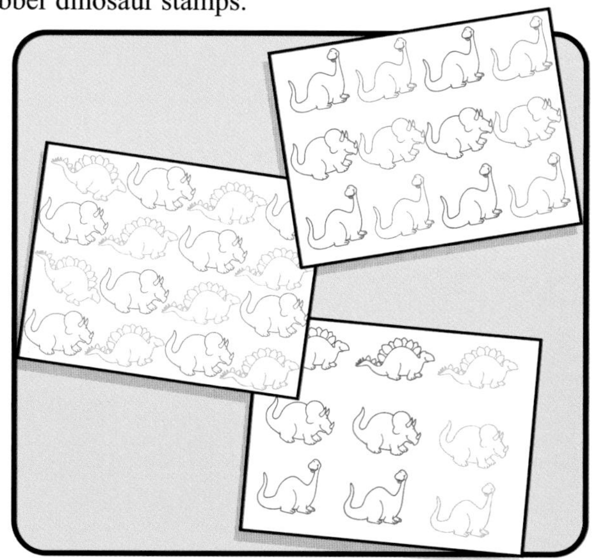

And Then There Were None!

Give each child in a small group ten small plastic dinosaurs. Have her place the dinosaurs in front of her in a straight line. Have her roll a die and subtract the number that she rolled from the line of dinosaurs. Have her lay these dinosaurs down on the table or floor to show they have been subtracted. Each child in the group takes turns until someone is able to subtract all of the dinosaurs from her line. To win, the child must roll the exact number needed to have all of the dinosaurs lying down.

LANGUAGE ARTS

What's In A Name?

Write several dinosaur names on individual strips of tagboard and laminate them for durability. Give each child in a small group a wipe-off marker and one of the dinosaur name strips. Place a stack of alphabet cards facedown. Have a child pick up the top card, call out the letter, and show it to the other children in the group. If a child has that letter in his dinosaur name, have him cross it out. Continue until one child has all of the letters crossed out. Wipe the strips clean with a paper towel, exchange the reshuffled alphabet cards, and begin the game again.

If I Had A Dinosaur

Have the class listen to and discuss the song "If I Had a Dinosaur" by Raffi on his *More Singable Songs* cassette or CD. Have each child think of one thing she could do if she had a dinosaur. After each child illustrates the idea on a sheet of drawing paper, have her dictate a sentence of explanation that begins with the same words as the song, "If I had a dinosaur, just think what…." Write the sentence on the picture. Glue the picture on a larger piece of construction paper and hang it in the classroom or hallway.

Dinosaur Words

Write the names of several dinosaurs on individual strips of tagboard to make matching pairs. Cut one of each name apart—letter by letter—and place the letters in individual resealable plastic bags. Give each child in a small group one of the bags along with the matching name card. Show the children how to use the letters to spell the dinosaur name. Demonstrate ways that some of the letters in the name can be used to spell shorter words. Have the children follow your example.

Dinosaur Stories

Begin the dinosaur unit by reading *Patrick's Dinosaurs* by Carol Carrick. This book will generate an interest in dinosaurs as it combines the fictional story of Patrick with several facts about some well-known dinosaurs. Follow up the story with a discussion about dinosaurs and their physical characteristics, habitats, and eating habits.

Conclude the unit with Carol Carrick's *What Happened To Patrick's Dinosaurs?* The sequel begins with Patrick's brother explaining a few of the theories about the extinction of dinosaurs and ends with Patrick sharing his own unique idea about their disappearance. Patrick's idea will inspire the children to think of some of their own ideas, which can be illustrated on drawing paper. Attach sentences of explanation dictated by the child to each drawing. The completed papers may be bound together to create a class book.

A Dinosaur Language Experience

Read *If The Dinosaurs Came Back* by Bernard Most. Discuss ways the author suggests dinosaurs could be used in the world today. Have the children think of other ways dinosaurs could be useful. Write their ideas on chart paper. Tape a large piece of white paper to a tabletop and have the children create a mural of their ideas. Copy the sentences from the chart paper onto the mural and display it in the classroom.

SCIENCE

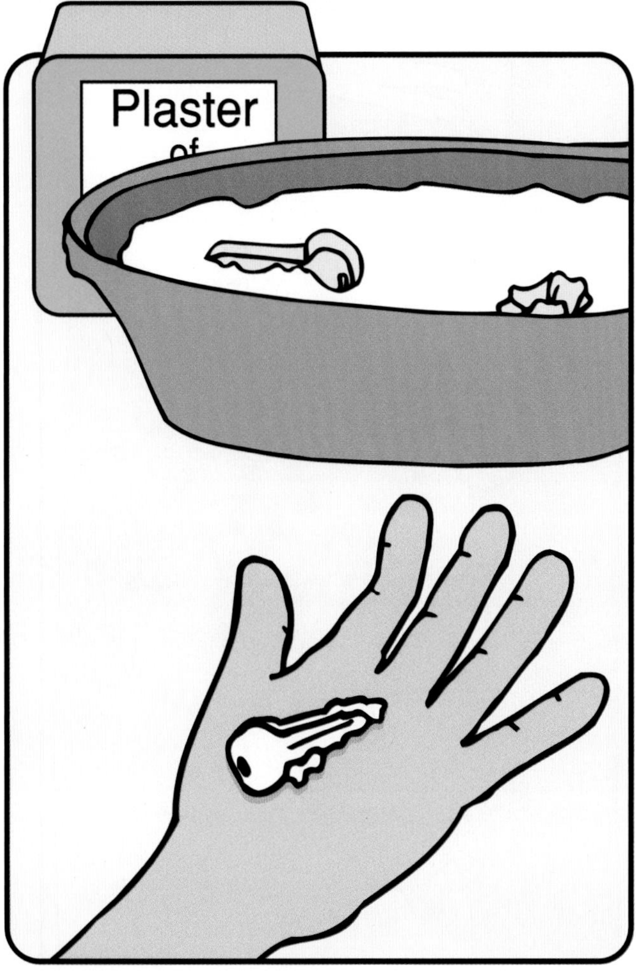

Fossils

Give each child in a learning center a pie tin. Have him press clay into the bottom of the tin until it reaches a one-inch thickness. Then have him make impressions in the clay using a number of small objects like rocks, keys, pinecones, hair combs, etc. Remove the objects from the clay and pour plaster of Paris over the clay to a one-inch thickness. Let the plaster dry according to package directions and then remove it from the clay and pie tin. This procedure represents the process by which fossils are formed.

Dinoland

Involve the entire class in the creation of Dinoland. Take your class outside to a sandbox. Divide the class into three or four groups. Have the children in each group work together to make a prehistoric land complete with hills, valleys, mountains, lakes, and volcanoes. Allow the children to use nearby rocks, leaves, and sticks to add to Dinoland. Have each group use a few plastic dinosaurs to complete its model.

Volcano

Have each child in a learning center participate in making baker's clay. Give each child a portion of the clay along with a small square of cardboard. Have each child use the clay to form a volcano on the cardboard. Have her use small rocks and sticks to decorate the base of the volcano. Allow the volcanoes to air-dry for three days or bake them at 300˚F for one hour.

Baker's Clay

1 cup salt
1½ cups warm water
food coloring
4 cups flour

Dissolve salt in warm water. To color the dough, add a few drops of food coloring. Allow the liquid mixture to cool, then add flour. Knead for ten minutes. See the directions above for how to finish these volcanoes.

SOCIAL STUDIES

Paleontologists

Fill plastic eggs (one or two more than the number of children in your class) with dinosaur stickers, and then bury the eggs in a sandbox. Take your class out to the sandbox and have the children dig in the sand to find the dinosaur eggs.

ART

Puzzlesaurus

Have each child color a copy of page 103. Next, have her cut apart the stegosaurus on the dotted lines. Then have her glue the four pieces of the stegosaurus puzzle to a piece of construction paper.

Bulletin Board

Draw the outlines of hills, mountains, plants, rocks, and a volcano on a large piece of white paper. Have a small group of children fill in the outlines with brightly colored paint. Once the paint is dry, staple the paper to a bulletin board. On individual sheets of paper, draw different dinosaurs. Have the children fill in the outlines with paint. When they're dry, cut out each dinosaur. Staple the dinosaurs to the bulletin board, leaving a small opening between each dinosaur and the background paper. Insert crumpled newspaper in the openings and then staple them shut. The result is an attractive 3-D bulletin board the children will love!

Mural

Cover a large tabletop with a piece of white paper. Tape the paper to the table's sides. Draw the outline of a dinosaur mural on the paper. Use a pencil and yardstick to divide the mural into squares (at least one per child). Give each child the opportunity to choose one square and color it with crayons, chalk, markers, or paint. The mural can be displayed in the classroom or hallway.

"Sock-a-saurus"

Have each child create a make-believe dinosaur from an old sock. The sock may be an adult's or a child's. It may be any color, but it must be clean! Provide materials such as ribbon, ricrac, yarn, pipe cleaners, etc., to decorate their socks. Children can insert their hands into the finished socks to create puppets or they may stuff them to make toys. Have each child share his sock-a-saurus with the class.

SNACK

Dinosaur Dig

small paper cups
plastic spoons
Ritz Dinosaurs Crackers
Fruit Loops cereal

Give each child a cup and a spoon. Have her place a dinosaur cracker in the bottom of the cup. Then let her fill the cup with the cereal. Ask her to eat the cereal down to the dinosaur.

CULMINATING ACTIVITY

Dinosaur Size

Help the children visualize the length of a dinosaur when doing this fun activity. Take the entire class out to the playground. Use a tape measure to determine the length of a particular dinosaur. Then have a number of children hold hands to show the length of the dinosaur. Demonstrate the lengths of other dinosaurs using the same procedure. Listed below are a few dinosaurs and their approximate lengths.

Brontosaurus (Apatosaurus)	70 feet
Tyrannosaurus	50 feet
Stegosaurus	25 feet
Ankylosaurus	15 feet
Compsognathus	2 feet

Dinosaur Puzzle

Use with "Tyrannosaurus" on page 95.

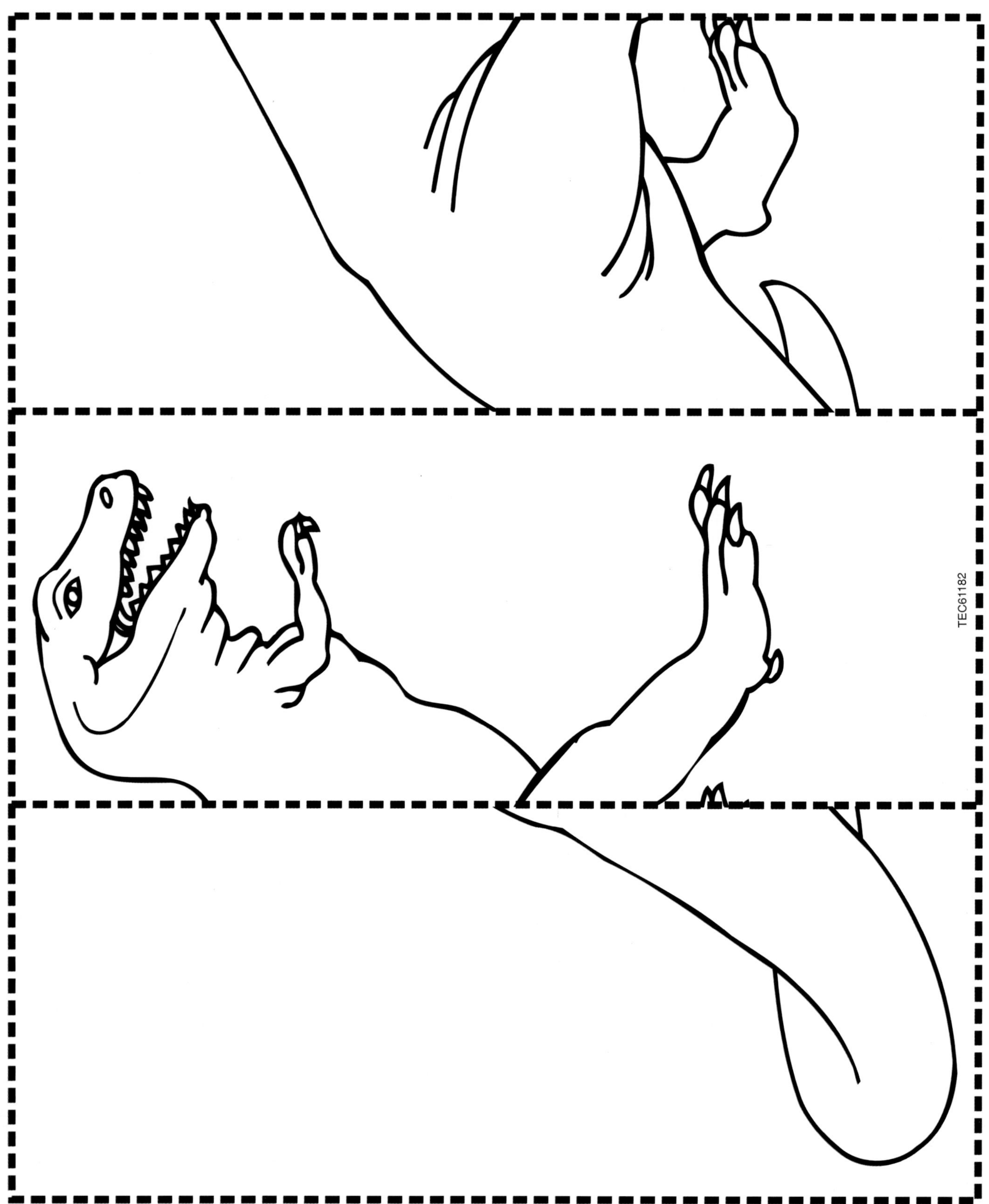

Use with "Puzzlesaurus" on page 100.

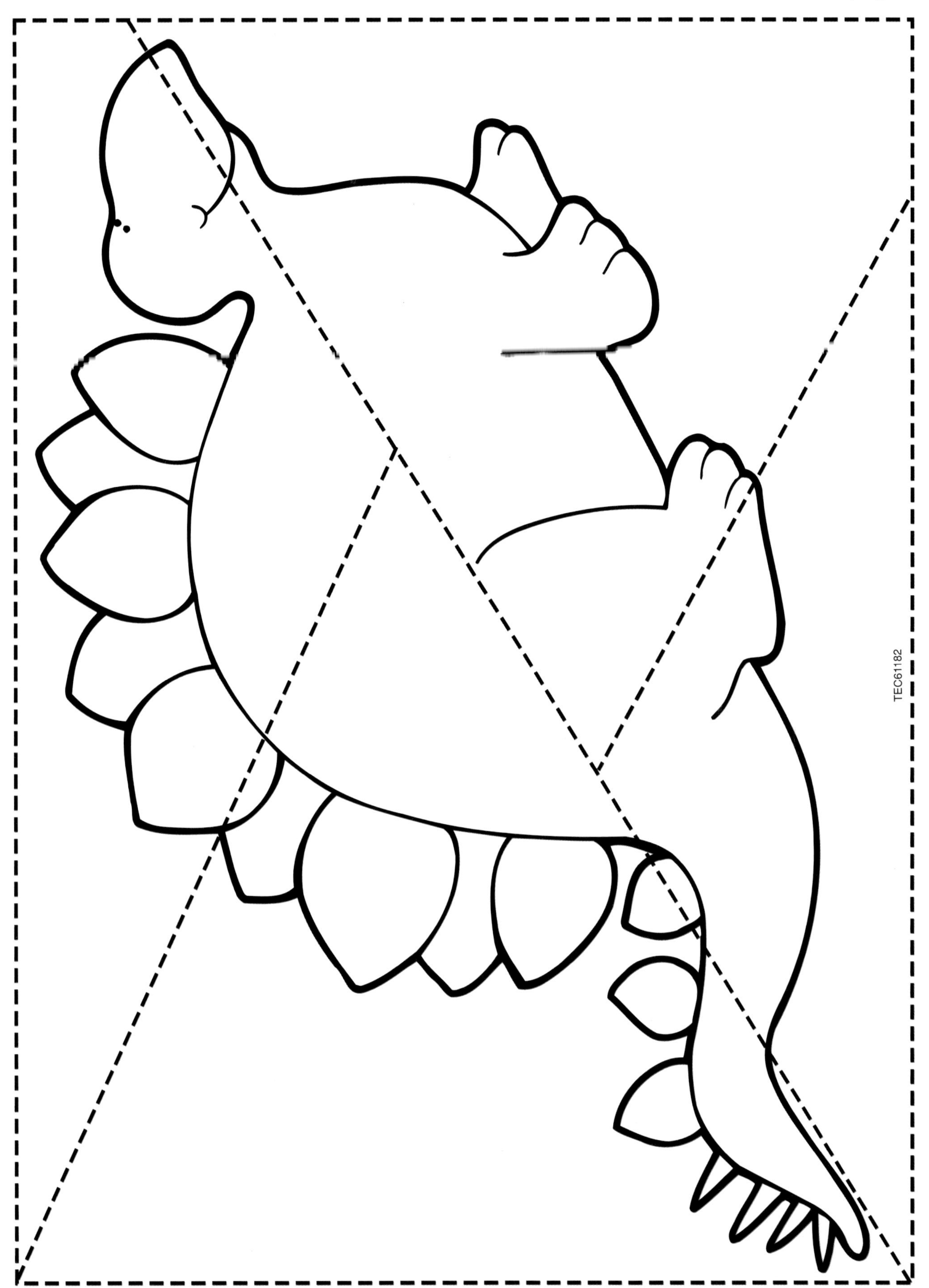

TEC61182

Pets

Most children have had experience with pets in their homes or in their neighborhoods. Giving children the opportunity to discuss, observe, and compare pets in the classroom will help them develop responsible attitudes toward other living things.

MATH

Pet Floor Graph

Make several copies of the pet cards on page 110 and place them in piles faceup on the floor. Read a word card with a pet name on it. If it is the name of a child's favorite pet, have her place a picture card next to the word card as shown. Repeat this step with each remaining name card. Then use the picture graph to compare the numbers of each type of pet.

Pet Patterning

Ready several copies of the pet cards from page 110 and place them in a learning center. Help the youngsters in the center use the cards to create patterns.

Fishing For Numbers!

Color, cut out, and laminate a copy of page 111. Place the game at a center and invite a child to place each fish on the corresponding fishbowl to match the numeral with the correct set.

Pets And Sets

Use pet items brought in by students to create sets of four. In each set place three things that go together and one thing that does not belong. Ask youngsters to look at each of the sets. Have them distinguish which of the items belong together and which does not. Have them give rationales for their choices.

Time Of Day

Create a time-of-day chart by using a marker to divide a piece of paper into three equal parts. Write one of the words *morning, afternoon,* and *evening* at the top of each part respectively. Duplicate the chart for each child. Ask each child to draw a picture of what a pet might do during that particular time of day.

Number Words

Write the numerals one, two, three, four, and five on the board. Under each numeral, write the corresponding number word. Encourage your youngsters to think of words that rhyme with each number word. Write the rhyming words under the number words. For older students, have each child choose a rhyming word for each number and draw a rhyming number/word picture for each pair. Bind the papers together to make individual books.

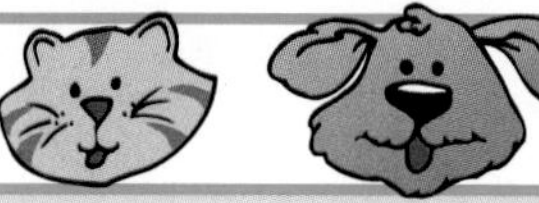
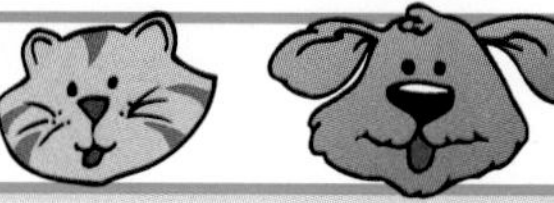

LANGUAGE ARTS

Pet Pals

After reading and discussing several books about pets, let each child tell about his pet. (Children who do not have pets may describe a pet that they would like to own.) Ask him to complete the sentence "My pet is a __________." Write each sentence on chart paper as it is dictated and add each child's name beside his response. Copy the sentences on individual pieces of paper. Give each child the piece of paper with his sentence written at the bottom. Have him illustrate the sentence. Bind the papers together to create a class book.

Word Wheel

In a small group, lead the children in a discussion about pets. Have each group choose one pet. Write the name of this pet in the center of a large piece of paper. Draw a circle around the pet name. Ask the youngsters to think of words that could describe the pet. Draw lines from the circle outward and write a descriptive word at the end of each line. Repeat the procedure for other pets. Then have each child choose one of the pets and draw a picture to illustrate the words shown in the word wheel. Attach the pictures to the appropriate word wheel.

Pondering Pets

Read the book *Dear Zoo* by Rod Campbell. This book will help youngsters think of reasons why certain animals make better pets than others. After reading the book, have the children brainstorm the characteristics of a good pet. Then have them think of animals that would make suitable pets.

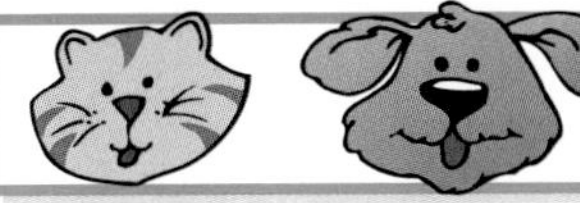

Class Book

Read Eric Carle's *Have You Seen My Cat?* Then have your youngsters use the same format as the book to write a book titled "Have You Seen My Pet?" Have one child draw an animal that would make a good pet. Write "This is my pet" below the drawing. Then have one child draw an animal that would not make a good pet. Write "This is not my pet" below that drawing. Continue in the same fashion. Bind the papers together to make a class book.

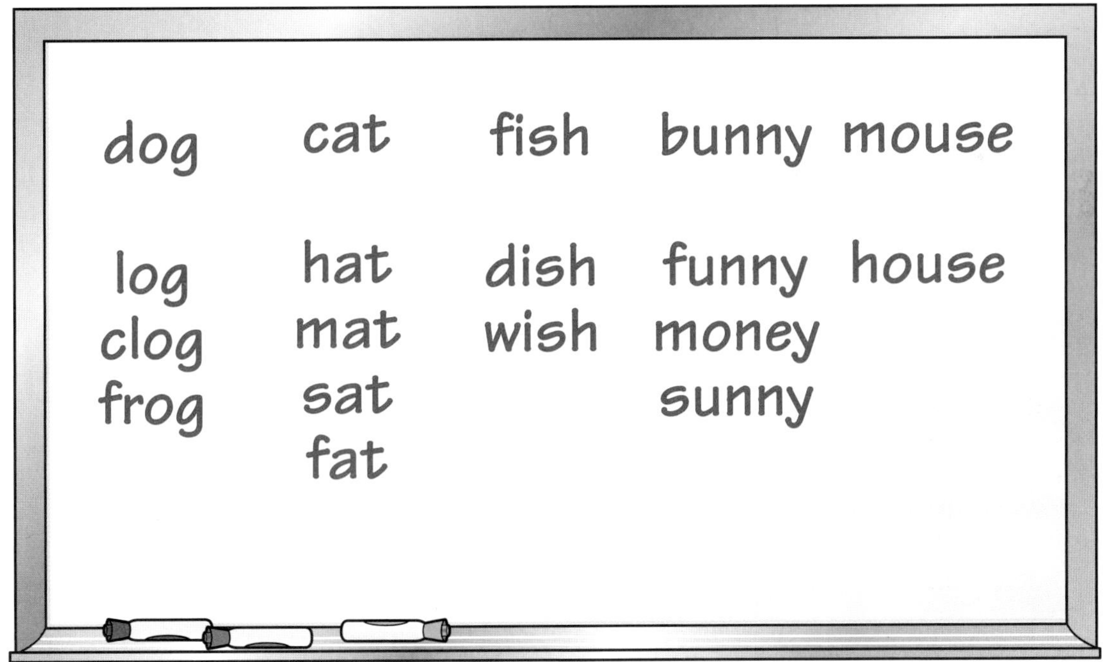

Rhyming Words

List the words *dog, cat, fish, bunny,* and *mouse* on the board. List words that rhyme with each of the pet names as your students dictate them. Then have your youngsters supply rhyming words to complete the following sentences:

I have a dog that jumps like a ___________.
I have a cat that wears a red ___________.
I have a fish that swims in a ___________.
I have a bunny that looks very ___________.
I have a mouse that lives in a ___________.

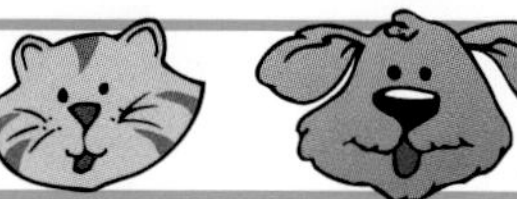
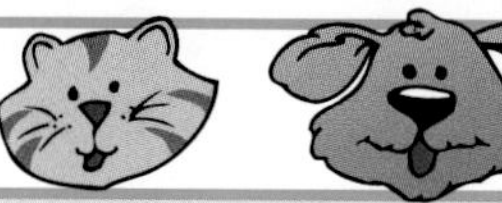

SCIENCE

Class Pet

Adopt a class pet such as a hamster, gerbil, turtle, or fish that can remain in the classroom throughout the school year. Discuss the proper care of this pet with the class. Each week, assign a child the responsibility of feeding and caring for the pet.

Thinking Exercise

Read the following sentences about pets and have your youngsters name each pet that you describe:

I am thinking of a pet that likes to drink milk and purrs when it is happy. *(cat)*

I am thinking of a pet that is green or brown and wears its house on its back. *(turtle)*

I am thinking of a pet that likes to eat carrots and has long ears. *(rabbit)*

I am thinking of a pet that wags its tail and barks. *(dog)*

SOCIAL STUDIES

Pet Needs

Discuss the basic needs of pets such as food, water, housing, grooming, exercise, and love. Discuss the various ways that these needs can be met by the owners of different kinds of pets.

Pet Store

Plan a field trip to a pet store. Ask the store attendant to describe the different types of pets and pet care items found in the store.

Class Pet Store

After the field trip to the pet store, set up a pet store in the classroom. Place a toy cash register, play money, stuffed animals, and pet care items in the classroom pet store. Have small groups of children take turns pretending that they are the store attendants and customers.

ART

Pet Masks

Have your youngsters create pet masks. To make a pet mask, give each child a paper plate. Have her paint one side of the plate with tempera paints. Allow the paint to dry. Then have her decorate the plate with facial features by using paper scraps, yarn, and feathers. Cut the eyes out of the mask so that youngsters will be able to see. Glue a tongue depressor to the bottom of each plate for the handle. Have your youngsters participate in a pet parade by holding their pet masks in front of their faces and marching around the classroom.

Thumbprint Pets

Place a few stamp pads and a supply of paper in a learning center. Ask each child to create several thumbprints by pressing her thumb in a stamp pad and then pressing it on a sheet of the paper. Then have her use a fine-line marker to draw features on each of the thumbprints to create different pets.

SNACK

Fruit Pets

Have each child create an original fruit pet. Give her a canned peach or pear half on a small paper plate. Then let her choose from a variety of foods to create the features. Toothpicks may be needed to attach some of the foods to the fruit.

1 canned peach or pear half for each child
1 small paper plate for each child
various foods for features, such as the following:

miniature marshmallows
pretzel sticks
cherries
chocolate chips

CULMINATING ACTIVITY

With permission from the school's principal or director, celebrate the conclusion of pet week with a pet show featuring class members and their pets. Arrange a time when parents can bring the pets to school. Pets suitable for a classroom setting may stay the entire day. Other pets should be scheduled to arrive at ten-minute intervals to avoid a number of pets being in the room at the same time.

Pet Cards

Use with "Pet Floor Graph" and "Pet Patterning" on page 104.

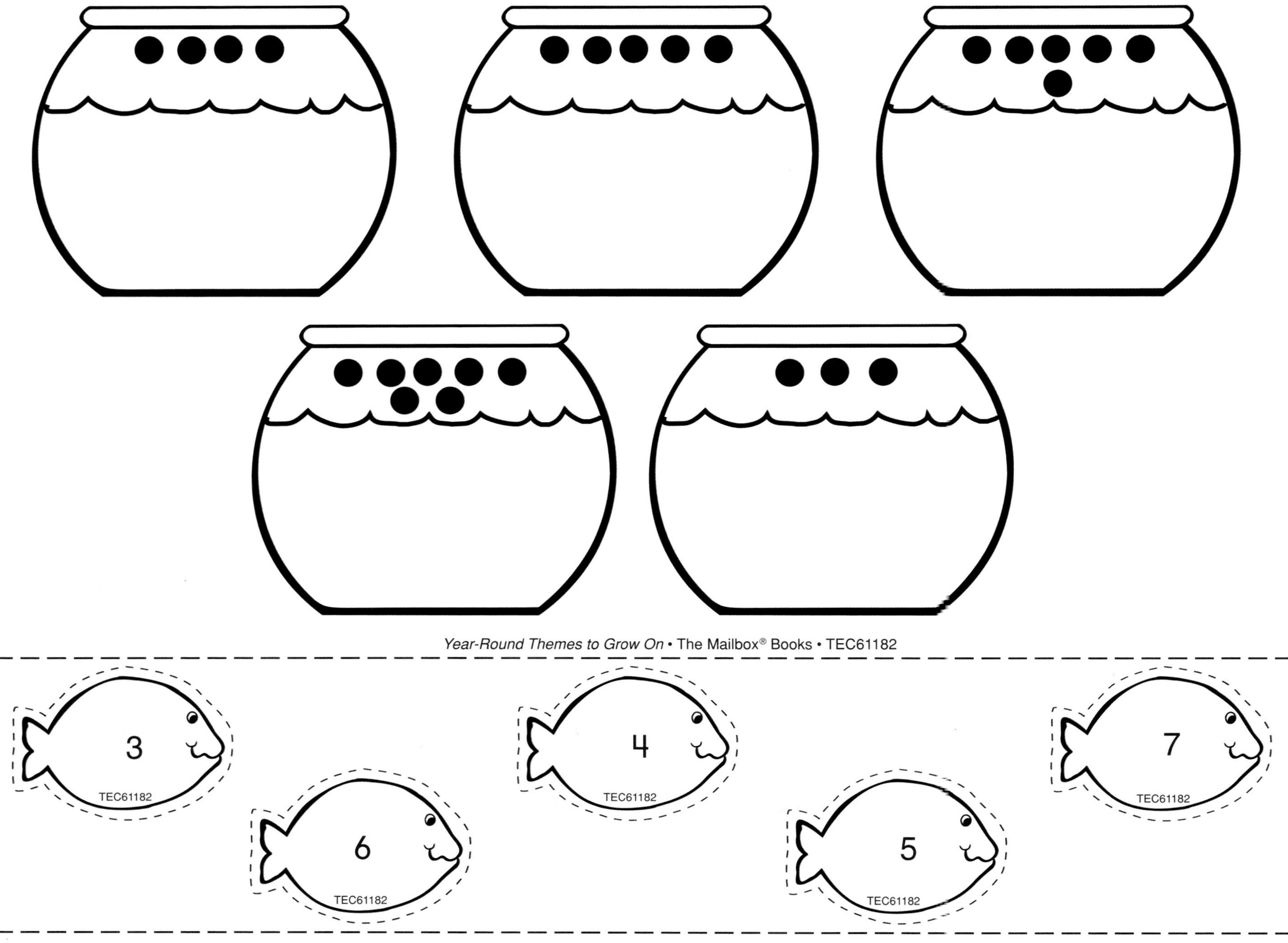

Note to the Teacher: Use with "Fishing for Numbers!" on page 104.

Spring Celebration

Watch your classroom come to life with these "egg-citing" springtime activities.

MATH

Sort And Count

Place a quantity of spring objects such as plastic eggs, toy chicks, silk flowers, and pieces of ribbon in a box. Use a marker to write the name of each object on a separate sheet of construction paper. Draw a simple picture of the object beside each name for easy identification. Then put the box of objects, the labeled sheets of paper, and several paper strips in a learning center. Let the children in the center sort the spring objects and place each one on the corresponding sheet of construction paper. For an added challenge, ask them to count each set of objects and then write the number and name of each set of objects on a paper strip.

Jelly Bean Estimation

Draw the outline of a jar on a large sheet of poster board, label with each child's name, and attach it to a wall. Next fill two small plastic jars with different amounts of jelly beans. Label one jar with the number of jelly beans inside. Place both jars on a small table in front of the poster. Have your youngsters carefully examine and compare the two jars of jelly beans. Then, based on her comparison, have each student estimate the number of jelly beans in the unlabeled jar. Write her estimation on a sticky note and attach it to the poster. At the end of the day, count the jelly beans in the unlabeled jar and decide which estimate was the closest. Repeat the activity every day of the unit, placing different amounts of jelly beans in each jar daily.

Simple Symmetry

Give each child a copy of page 120. Then have him complete the pictures of the bunny and Easter egg.

One Dozen

Set up a general store in a learning center. Place a toy cash register, craft foam circles (pennies), shopping bags, and several items such as plastic eggs and toy chicks in the center. Invite the children to take turns playing the customers and store clerk. Have the customers choose any combination of a dozen items, place the items in shopping bags, and purchase the items from the clerk with 12 pennies. Have the clerk count the money and the items in each shopping bag. Then ask the children to switch roles and repeat the activity.

Egg Carton Match

Label each section of a foam egg carton (cleaned and sanitized) with a number 1 to 12. Also label each of 12 plastic eggs with a number 1 to 12 and place them in a basket. Invite a child from a small group to close her eyes and pick an egg from the basket. Then have her place the egg in the section of the egg carton with the matching number. Have her pass the basket to the next child. Continue in the same manner with the remaining eggs.

Egg Timer

Have a small group of students sit in a circle. Give each child a plastic spoon. Designate one child as the starter and give her a plastic egg. Have the children pass the egg around the circle clockwise using only their spoons. Time the activity with a three-minute timer. Count the number of times the egg is passed around the circle in a three-minute period. When the game is over, choose another child to be the starter, and begin again.

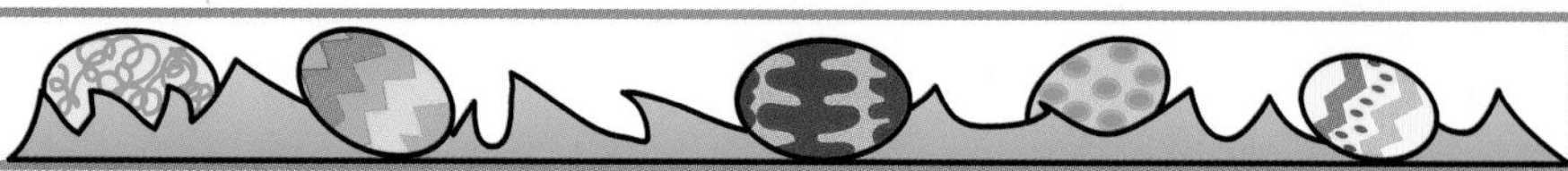

LANGUAGE ARTS

It's Spring

Read aloud *The Tale Of Peter Rabbit* by Beatrix Potter. Then give each child a strip of paper that has been folded into fourths. Review the story, and then have her draw pictures showing the sequence of events.

Spring Words

Fold a quantity of 9" x 12" sheets of construction paper in half. Then assign each child in a small group a different spring word. Have him write or copy the word on the left side of the paper and illustrate it. On the right side, have him write or dictate words that describe the spring word and picture.

ABC Bunny Words

Help your children brainstorm several bunny words such as *hop, tail, ears, nose, pink, fur, carrot, bunny, lettuce, rabbit, garden, jump, whiskers,* and *vegetables.* Write the words on a large bunny cutout. Then copy each word on an individual word card along with a picture cue, and place the cards in a learning center. Help the children in the center put the bunny words in alphabetical order using the first letter.

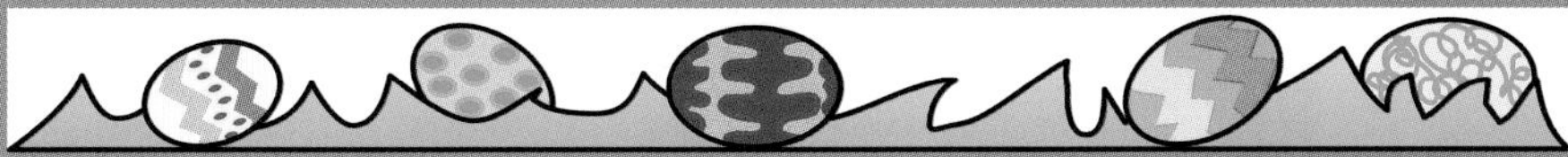

Springtime Journal

Make a journal for each child by stapling five sheets of paper inside a bright-colored paper cover. Each day have her use the journal to record the date and at least one sign of spring observed that day. Let younger children draw pictures of their daily observations.

Missing Letters

Give each child a copy of page 121. Have her fill in the missing letters of the alphabet. Provide an alphabet chart to use as a guide.

Spring Categories

Have your children think of items that belong in the categories shown below. List each item under the appropriate heading. Then make several blank booklets by stapling three white pages inside each bright-colored paper cover. Place the booklets and the lists in a learning center. Let each child in the center choose a booklet and a category. Have him copy the name of the category on the front cover. Then, on each page of the booklet, have him copy the name of one item in the category and draw a picture of it. Leave the booklets in the center until all of them are complete.

Things That Hop
Things That Bloom
Things With Fur
Things With Whiskers
Things That Are Sweet
Things That Are Soft
Things With Feathers
Things That Hatch

Jennie's Hat

Read aloud *Jennie's Hat* by Ezra Jack Keats. Have your children name all of the things in the book that Jennie uses as a hat. Print the name of each object in the correct order on a sheet of chart paper. Next have your youngsters name the objects brought by the birds to decorate Jennie's hat. List the name of each in the correct order on the same sheet of chart paper. Then demonstrate how each child can make a hat using two strips of wrapping paper or newsprint (see "Spring Bonnet" on page 118).

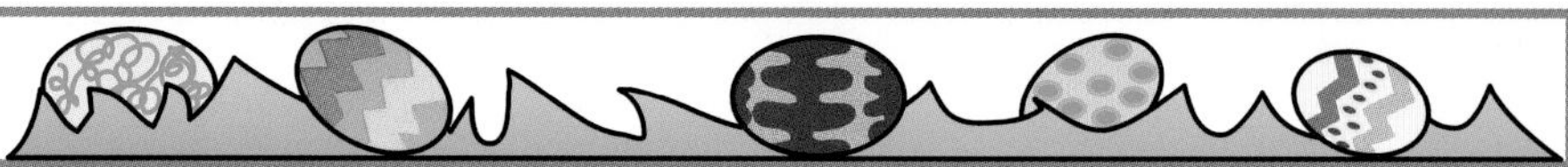

SCIENCE

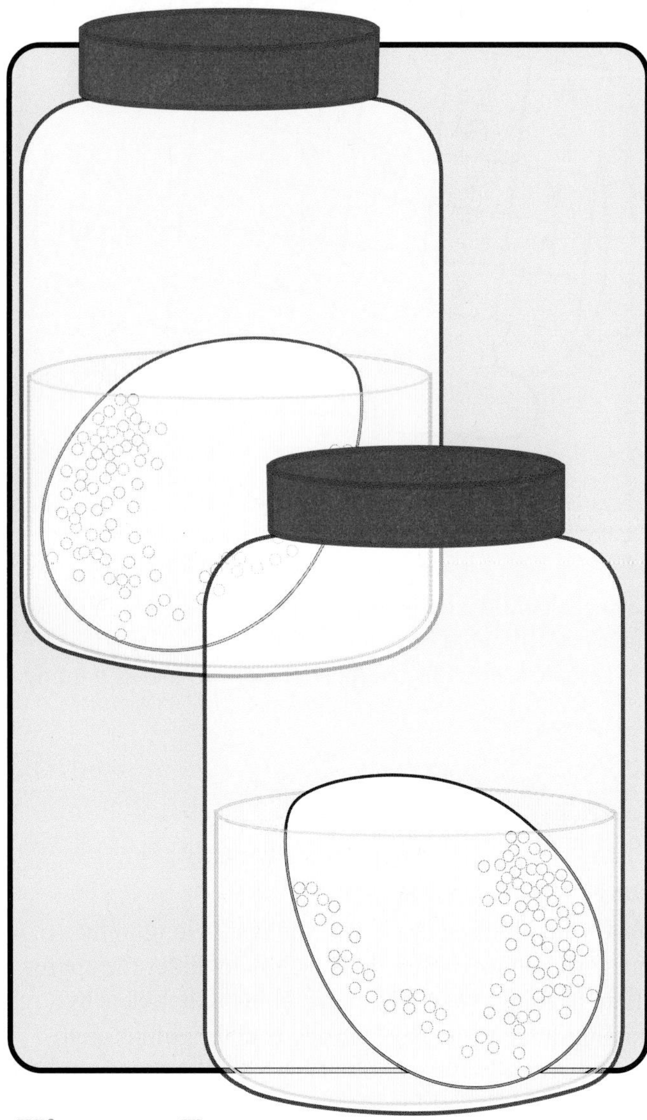

Vinegar Egg

Place a raw egg in a plastic container filled with vinegar. Seal the container tightly. The vinegar will slowly dissolve the calcium shell and rubberize the egg. Have your children observe the changes in the egg daily. In approximately two days, the shell will begin to soften and disappear. On the third day, take the egg out of the vinegar and let your youngsters hold it. The shell will be completely dissolved, and the egg will look and feel like a balloon filled with jelly.

Spring Walk

Take a nature walk with your children. Have them look for animals, flowers, trees, insects, and signs of spring while on the walk. When you return to the classroom, ask each child to draw a picture of one thing she saw outside. When your youngsters have finished their drawings, let them share what they saw with the others in the classroom. Bind the drawings together to create a class book or use them to make an attractive bulletin-board display called "Signs Of Spring."

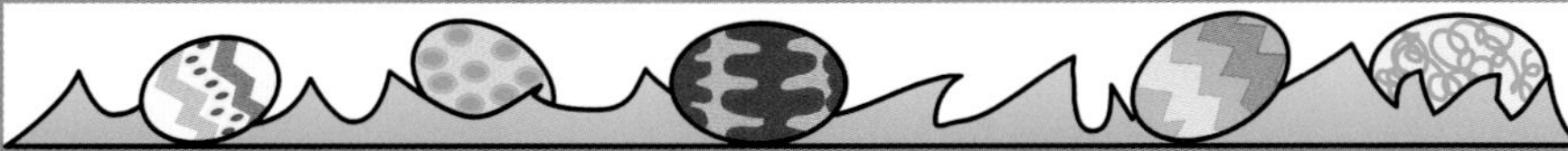

SOCIAL STUDIES

Egg Roll

One of the oldest Washington, D.C., traditions is the egg-rolling event held on Easter Monday on the South Lawn of the White House. The event was first held on the grounds of the Capitol. Each year children came to test their rolling skills. However, during the Hayes administration, several congressmen grew tired of the mess created by the egg roll and banned it from the Capitol grounds. President and Mrs. Hayes invited the children to come to the White House, and the egg roll has since remained a tradition.

After sharing this brief history of the event, let your children participate in their own egg-rolling contest. Have each child decorate a hard-boiled egg. Then take your children outside to the playground. Mark off a starting line and a finish line. Divide the class into several small groups. Have each child in a small group place his egg at the starting line and roll it with his hands to the finish line. Repeat the activity for each small group.

We've Changed!

After discussing the many changes that occur during spring, let your children participate in an activity to see how they have changed. Ask each child to bring a baby picture from home. Post the baby pictures on a bulletin board. Then write each child's name on a strip of tagboard and place the strips in a container. Let small groups of students take turns matching names to faces. Have the children use Sticky-Tac to attach the name cards under the pictures. Then return the names to the container when the group has finished so another group can have a turn. Finally assemble the youngsters around the bulletin board and let each child match her name to her baby picture.

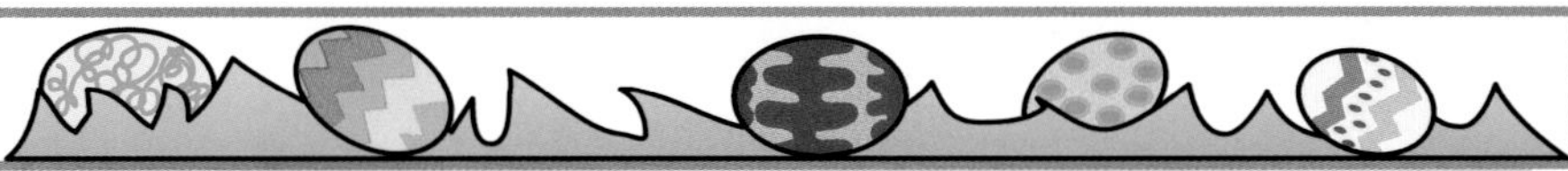

ART

Springtime Butterfly

To make a butterfly, have each student draw or trace an outline of a butterfly on white paper, using as much of the paper as possible. Spray thinned tempera paint from a spray bottle over the butterfly drawing. Allow the paint to dry. Have the student cut out the butterfly. Hang these delightful works of art in your classroom.

Bunny Ears

Let each child make a pair of bunny ears to wear for the Bunny Party (see page 119). Place scissors, pink tempera paint, sponges, a paper puncher, white construction paper, bunny ear patterns, and several plastic headbands in a learning center. Have each child trace two ear patterns on white construction paper and then cut them out. Then have her sponge-paint the inside of each ear pink. At the bottom of each ear, punch two holes large enough for the headband to go through. Then thread the headband through the four holes.

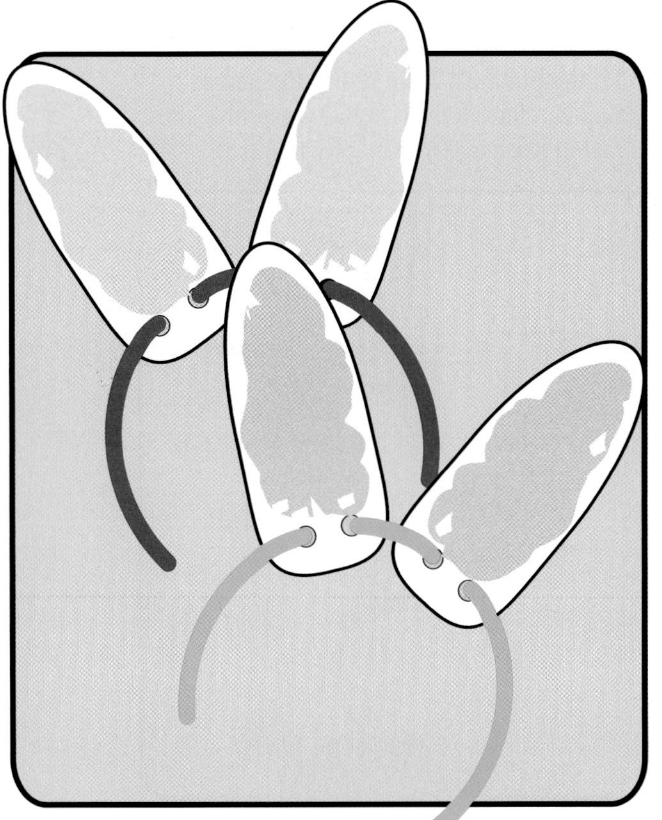

Torn-Paper Bunny

Place colored paper, glue, tagboard squares, several plastic lids of various sizes, and markers in a learning center. To make a bunny, a child chooses a large lid and a small one. He places one lid on a small piece of colored paper and tears the paper around the outside edge to create a circle. He repeats the procedure with the second lid. Then he glues the two circles on a piece of tagboard to make the body of the bunny. He tears paper ears and a tail, and glues the features to the bunny's body. He uses a marker to draw the whiskers. Chicks, ducklings, and other spring animals can be made using the same procedure.

Spring Bonnet

Cut two 2-foot strips from wrapping paper or newsprint. Lay the strips of paper over the child's head in the form of a cross. Then wrap masking tape around the outside of the paper at the crown of the head. Next begin at one end of the paper and roll tightly toward the masking tape. Continue around the hat until all four sides have been rolled up to form a brim. Wrap and glue a strip of construction paper or a piece of crepe paper around the masking tape to make a hatband. Then decorate the hat with a variety of materials such as sequins, feathers, and paper flowers.

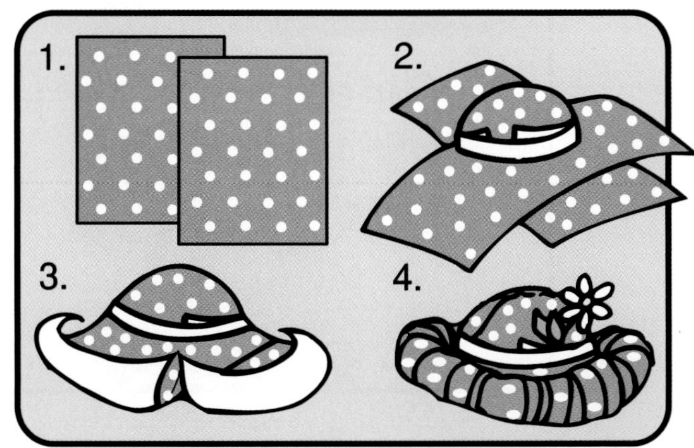

SNACK

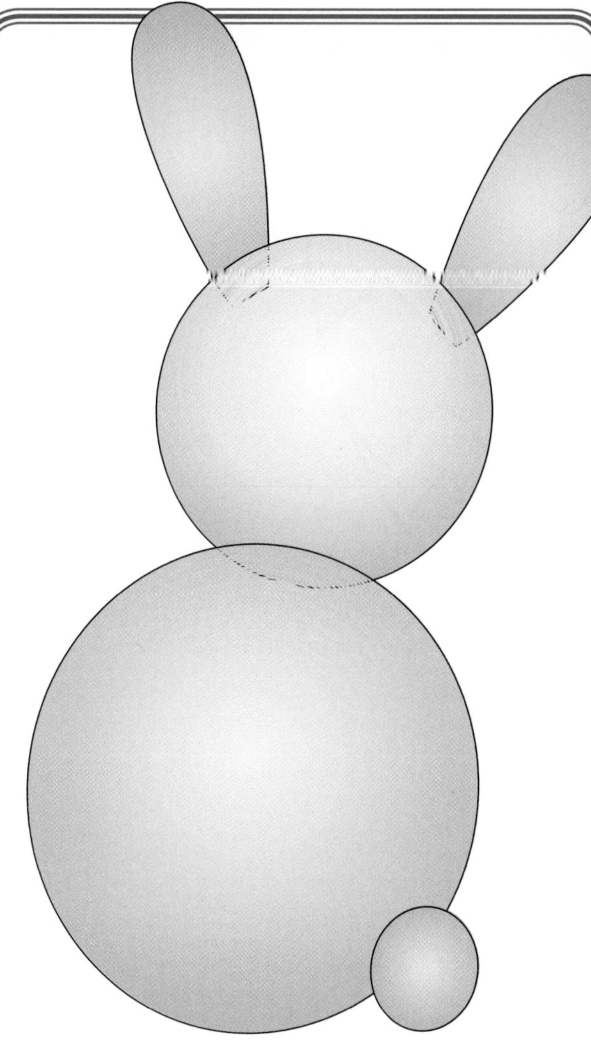

Bunny Bread

Prepare a loaf of frozen bread dough. Let the dough thaw. Then divide it in half. Shape one half into a flattened circle for the bunny's body and place it on a lightly greased cookie sheet. Divide the second half into two equal parts. Use one half to make the bunny's head and place next to the body. Then use the remainder to make the ears and tail. Cover and let rise for approximately 20 minutes. Then bake at 400 degrees for 18 minutes.

CULMINATING ACTIVITY

Bunny Party

Begin the party by playing the game Bunny Relay. Program a chart as shown giving a picture cue for which bunny facial part comes first, second, etc. Divide the class into groups of six. Post the chart so all teams can see it. Then draw a bunny body on the board for each team for the children to use as a guide. Next have each team line up single file approximately ten feet from the board. Give the first child on each team a piece of chalk. Call out the first facial part and have each of these children hop on both feet to the board and draw a circle to make the bunny's head. The first player then hops back to his team and hands the chalk to the next child. The next team member draws the bunny ears. Guide children by calling out each facial part to be drawn. Play continues until each part of the bunny's face is drawn in order. If desired have each child don his bunny ears (from "Bunny Ears" on page 118) during the game.

Egg and Bunny Patterns

Use with "Simple Symmetry" on page 112.

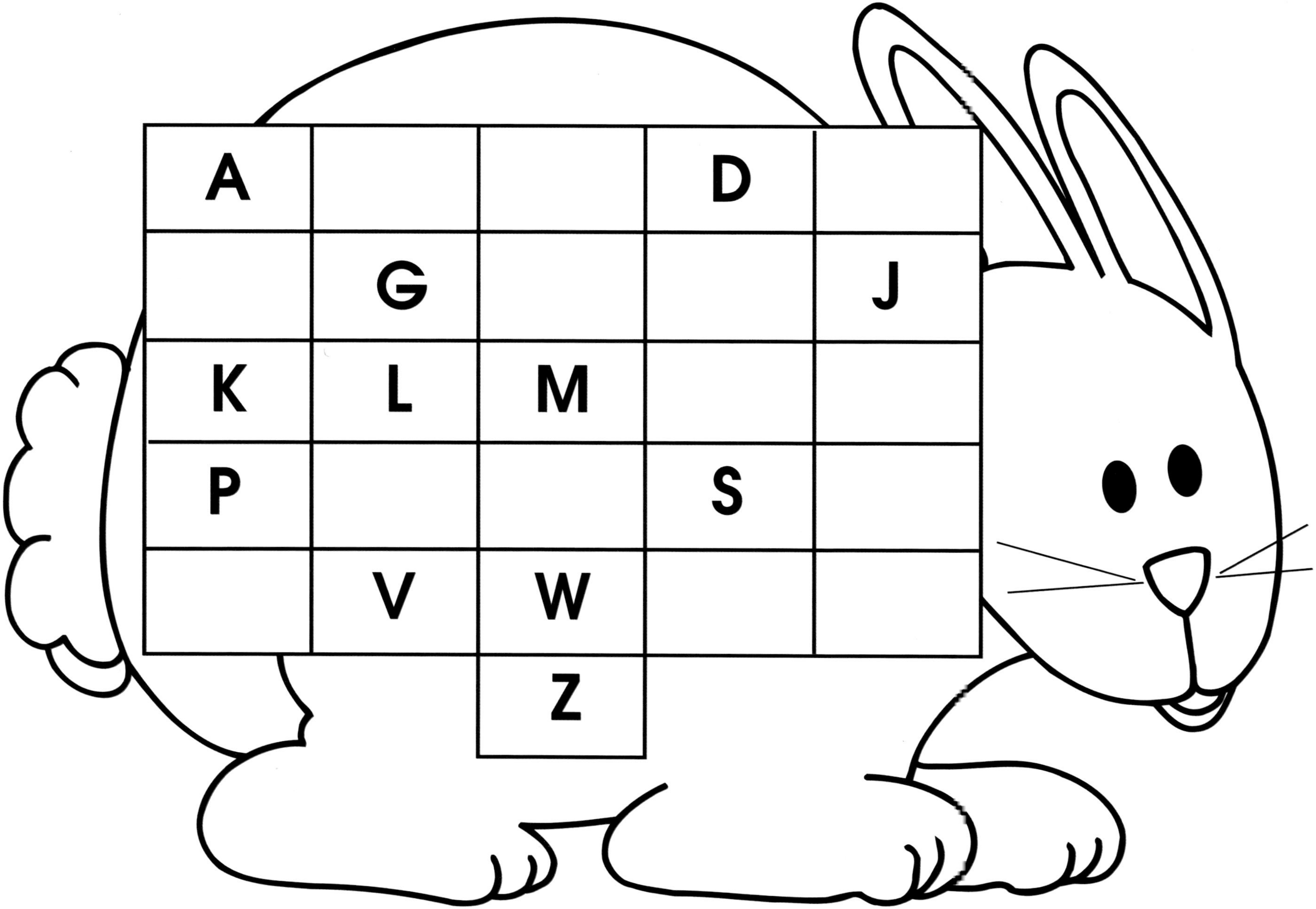

A			D	
	G			J
K	L	M		
P			S	
	V	W		
		Z		

Note to the teacher: Use with "Missing Letters" on page 115.

Over In The Meadow

Acquaint your children with the animals at the forest's edge as you stretch their awareness with these fun-to-do meadow activities.

MATH

Shell Game

Invite a small group of children to sit around a table. Give each child a bowl. Ask her to pretend it is a turtle's shell. Also give her five small blocks. Have her place the shell upside down over the blocks. Then have her remove two blocks from under the shell and place them beside it as shown. Ask her to tell how many blocks are left under the shell. Have her lift the shell to check her answer. Continue the activity in the same manner, asking each child to place different combinations of blocks underneath and beside the shell.

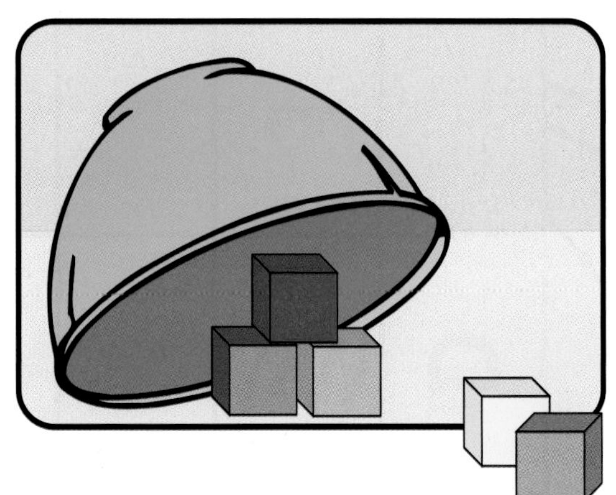

Meadow Math

Create a meadow scene on a bulletin board. To do this, begin by covering the board with green paper. Use blue paper to make a pond and mount it on the green background. Complete the scene by adding flowers and sprigs of grass made from paper scraps. Make several bunny, butterfly, turtle, and fish cutouts. Each day, mount a different number of animals on the bulletin board. Ask your children questions similar to those listed below.

How many fish do you see?

How many bunnies do you see?

Are there more bunnies than fish? How many more?

Then give each child a copy of the bar graph on page 130. Have him color the boxes to show the number of each animal on the board.

Greater Than/Less Than

Give each child a copy of page 131. Ask her to write a numeral that is less than each set of meadow animals in the less-than column and a numeral that is greater than each set in the greater-than column. To vary the activity for younger children, ask them to draw or use stamps to show an appropriate number of meadow animals in each column.

Ordering Earthworms

Cut a quantity of different lengths of yarn or brown ribbon, place them in a container, and label it "Earthworms." Invite each child in a small group to take five "earthworms" from the container and place them on a mat in order from the shortest to the longest. Then have him place them back into the container and repeat the process with five more earthworms.

How Many Babies?

How many baby animals are in the book *Over In The Meadow* illustrated by Ezra Jack Keats? Read the book aloud to your children. Then let each child estimate how many babies are in the meadow. Record each student's estimation on a slip of paper. Read the book again, stopping after each verse to tally the number of babies. At the conclusion of the story, total the number of tally marks. Then ask each child to compare his estimation with the total to determine who came the closest.

Leapfrog

Use the game of Leapfrog to reinforce the position words *beside*, *behind*, *between*, and *front*. Ask several student volunteers to position themselves as frogs ready to leap. Direct one child to leap beside a second child. Tell a third child to leap behind another. Continue the game in the same fashion until each word has been illustrated. Then divide the class into small groups. Have your children listen to your directions and play Leapfrog in groups. To vary the activity, play Leapfrog using ordinal positions.

LANGUAGE ARTS

Busy Beavers

Read the book *Building Beavers* by Kathleen Martin-James. Write the sound words *crunch, plop, splash,* and *thump* on separate index cards. Have children think of ways these sounds can be made. Place the index cards, paper, pencils, and crayons in a center. Invite each child to copy each word on a separate sheet of paper and draw a picture of something that might create that sound. Bind each child's pages together inside a bright-colored cover to make individual books titled "Sound Words."

Animal ABC Order

Have older students try this activity to reinforce alphabetizing. Print each of the following meadow animal names on individual word cards: *ant, beaver, chipmunk, deer, earthworm, frog, grasshopper, lizard, mouse, owl, rabbit, snail, turtle,* and *wasp*. Place the word cards in a learning center. Ask the children in the center to put the names in alphabetical order.

"Little White Duck"

Have students listen to "Little White Duck" by Raffi from the CD *Everything Grows.* Next ask four volunteers to act out the song while you play it again. Then give each child a copy of the sequence cards on page 130. Have him cut apart the picture cards and glue them on the remaining numbered strip in the proper sequence in which they appear in the song.

"The Frog On The Log"

Your children will enjoy the repetitive rhythm of the delightful "The Frog On The Log" by Ilo Orleans from *Read-Aloud Rhymes For The Very Young* selected by Jack Prelutsky. Print the poem on a sheet of chart paper. Use the chart to teach the poem to your children. Then divide the class into six groups. Assign each group one stanza of the poem and guide them in reading it chorally as a poem.

Waddle Or Wiggle?

Waddle, wiggle, slither, hop, crawl—your children can do them all! But what about a lizard or a duck? Make a list of meadow animals on a sheet of chart paper. Then have your children think of one word to describe how each animal moves. Print the movement word beside each animal's name. Let each child choose an animal and demonstrate how it would move.

Reading Fun

Read aloud the book *If You Give A Mouse A Cookie* by Laura Joffe Numeroff. Then review the story with students and make a list of each item asked for by the mouse. As a followup activity, gather an example of each item on the list. Place the items in random order on the floor. Reread the book, stopping to ask youngsters what the mouse will ask for next. Invite volunteers to place the items in sequential order as they are named.

City	Country
apartment town house house	house farm ranch
car taxi subway	truck tractor horse
tuxedo suit dress	jeans overalls straw hat
fast foods	fresh fruit milk vegetables

Opposite Mice

Read aloud "City Mouse—Country Mouse" from *City Mouse—Country Mouse And Two More Mouse Tales From Aesop* illustrated by John Wallner. Ask your children to listen for opposites in the text and look for opposites in the illustrations as you read. Then write the words "City" and "Country" at the top of a sheet of chart paper. Have youngsters name the different types of housing, food, clothing, transportation, and animals found in the city and in the country. Record student responses on the chart. Afterward ask each child if he would rather be a city mouse or a country mouse, and have him explain why.

Act It Out

The descriptive language used in *The Snail's Spell* by Joanne Ryder makes it an excellent book for dramatic play. Read the book aloud to your class. Then reread it and ask each child to pretend to be the snail and act out the story.

SCIENCE

Camouflage

Many meadow animals—such as toads, lizards, and rabbits—match the color of their surroundings to help them hide from their enemies. Tell your children that the term for this special ability is *camouflage*. Then invite youngsters to participate in a camouflage game. To prepare, cut several strips of matching construction paper, wrapping paper, and/or wallpaper. Tape some of the strips to objects that are different colors and others to objects that are the same color. Show your children an example of a paper strip they are to find. Then let them look around the room. Each time a strip is found, attach it to a sheet of poster board. Once all the strips have been located, discuss why some were easier to find than others.

Beaver Dam

Help your students create a model of a beaver dam. First cut a hole in the center of a heavy sheet of cardboard. Then paint the cardboard blue to resemble water and let it dry. To make the beaver lodge, place a large bowl upside down over the hole. Cover the bowl with a layer of clay. Press small sticks and twigs into the clay. Next read aloud *Building Beavers* by Kathleen Martin-James. Afterward let small groups of children take turns reenacting the story using stick puppets and the beaver dam model.

Classroom Critters

Most children are familiar with the small mammals often kept as classroom pets such as gerbils, mice, guinea pigs, and hamsters. During this unit, introduce your children to other classroom critters such as snails, crickets, grasshoppers, earthworms, turtles, and frogs. These animals can be found in pet stores, bait shops, or your own backyard. They require little care and can be returned to their natural environment once you are finished with them.

How Animals Move

Print the words *crawl, walk, swim,* and *fly* at the top of individual sheets of poster board. Ask your youngsters to name animals that move in one of the four ways. Then have them cut out pictures of animals from nature magazines and attach them to the appropriate posters.

SOCIAL STUDIES

Fears

Everyone is afraid of something. In the book *Franklin In The Dark* by Paulette Bourgeois, Franklin, a turtle, will not go into his shell because he is afraid of the dark. Read the story aloud to your youngsters. Then have them name the other animals in the book and their fears. Next have the children describe what each animal does to overcome its fear. Conclude the discussion by asking each child to name something that frightens him. Encourage your children to think of ways to help each other overcome their fears.

Who Lives Here?

Each type of meadow animal lives in the home that best meets its needs. Show your youngsters photographs of animal homes from factual books and describe the features that make them unique. Then play Who Lives Here? To play this game, describe an animal home and ask your children to name the animal that lives there.

Field Trip

Plan a field trip to a state or national park, and take your youngsters on a nature hunt for small meadow animals and their homes. Then enjoy a picnic lunch before you return to school. If your school is not located near a park, invite a park ranger to visit your classroom and discuss her work with animals.

Rules

Peter Rabbit's mother told him not to go into Mr. McGregor's garden. But Peter disobeyed his mother and got into a lot of trouble. Read aloud *The Tale Of Peter Rabbit* by Beatrix Potter. Then discuss why rules are important. Have your children help you list several safety rules such as "Never play with matches," "Don't talk to strangers," and "Look both ways before crossing the street." Then ask them to describe what could happen if each of the rules was not obeyed.

ART

Torn-Paper Turtle

Invite each child in a small group to use a pattern to trace a turtle shape on a sheet of green or brown construction paper. Have him cut out the turtle. Then glue bright-colored pieces of torn paper on its back to make a decorative shell.

Fish Puppets

Help each child trace around his hand on a piece of tagboard; then cut it out. Have him use markers or paints to decorate the cutout so it resembles a fish. Then attach a craft stick to the back to create a fish puppet.

Meadow Animals

Have your children follow these simple, step-by-step directions to draw meadow animals.

Baby Birds In A Nest

1. Draw a half-circle.
2. Draw three small circles on top of the half-circle.
3. Add an eye and a beak to each circle.

Duck In A Pond

1. Draw an oval.
2. Draw a small circle on top of the oval.
3. Add an eye, a beak, and a tail.
4. Make wavy lines for the water.

Turtle

1. Draw a half-circle.
2. Draw a small circle on the end of the half-circle.
3. Add an eye, a tail, and legs.

SNACK

Owl Eyes

Freeze a tube of slice-and-bake sugar cookie dough for one hour. Remove the wrapper and slice the frozen dough into ¼-inch slices. Give each child in a small group two slices. Have her overlap them slightly on an ungreased cookie sheet. Press the two slices together. Then push a chocolate chip into the center of each slice of dough to create the eyes. Bake at 350° for 12 minutes. Then, press a triangle-shaped cracker between the eyes to make the beak.

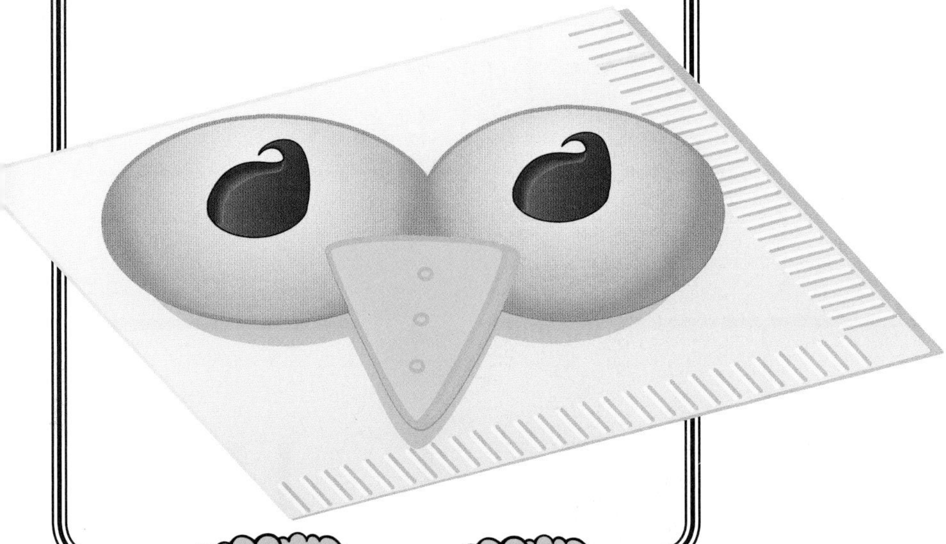

CULMINATING ACTIVITY

Meadow Mural

Have your children work together to create an attractive meadow mural. Cover a bulletin board with white paper. Draw a meadow scene on the paper. Include trees, grass, a pond, the sun, logs, and rocks. Then let small groups of children take turns painting the scene. Ask other small groups to use construction-paper scraps, markers, and crayons to make the meadow animals. Attach the animals to the scene to complete the mural.

Bar Graph

Use with "Meadow Math" on page 122.

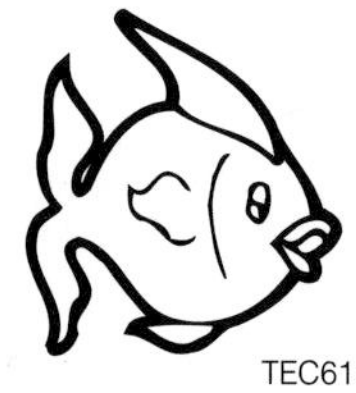 TEC61182					

Sequence Cards

Use with " 'Little White Duck' " on page 124.

1	2	3	4
 TEC61182		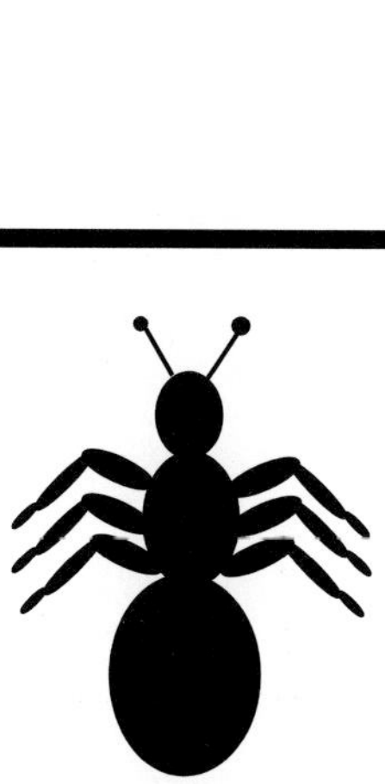	

Less		More

	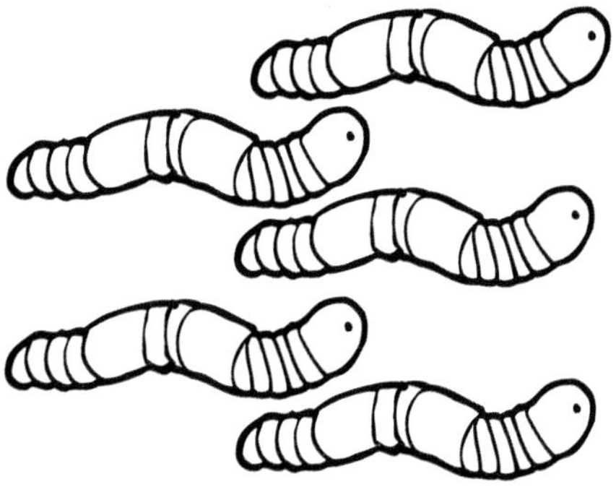	

Note to the teacher: Use with "Greater Than/Less Than" on page 123.

Insects And Spiders

Adjust your safari hat and binoculars as you embark on an insect and spider adventure. Observations of these creatures will open doors for your youngsters' increased knowledge and wonder about insects and spiders.

MATH

Bugs In A Jar

Place several plastic bugs in a plastic jar. Then write the correct number of bugs in the jar and two other random numbers (perhaps one number greater than and one less than the actual number) on a piece of folded paper as shown. Place the bug jar, folded paper, scraps of paper, a pencil, and another plastic jar on a table. Ask each child to estimate how many bugs are in the jar. Tell them the correct number is one of the three numbers printed on the folded paper. Help each child write his name and estimation on a slip of paper and place it in the empty jar. Next, have students count aloud as you remove the bugs from the jar. Then pull out the slips to determine how many children chose the correct number. Finally repeat the activity, placing a different number of bugs in the jar.

"The Ants Go Marching"

Lead your class in singing "The Ants Go Marching…" Then give each child ten black construction paper circles. Tell her to pretend the circles are ants. Ask the following subtraction questions and have her use the ants to help find the answers:

If there are 10 ants and 2 march down into the ground, how many are left? *(8)*

If 1 more ant marches down into the ground, how many are left? *(7)*

If 2 more ants march down into the ground, how many are left? *(5)*

If 4 more ants march down into the ground, how many are left? *(1)*

If 1 more ant marches down into the ground, how many are left? *(0)*

Bugs! Bugs! Bugs!

Ask your children to help you create a list of bugs. Then ask each child to choose one bug from the list and copy it onto his paper. Have him draw a picture of it using his imagination and basic knowledge of the bug. Finally graph the bug drawings to see which ones were drawn the most, the least, and not at all.

Caterpillars

Give each child a sheet of yellow construction paper, glue, and five different-colored circles cut from orange, red, purple, green, and blue construction paper. Tell her to follow your directions for making a colorful caterpillar. On the yellow construction paper, have her glue the orange circle on first, the red circle second, the purple circle third, and so on. Then let her use crayons or paper scraps to add features to the caterpillar. Afterward, ask her to name the ordinal position of each circle.

How Many Bugs?

Prepare a book for each child by inserting five blank pages inside a cover and writing the title "How Many Bugs?" on the front. Place the books, markers, a stamp pad, rubber insect stamps, and spider stamps in a center. Help each child write a different number on each of the five pages. Then have him use the rubber stamps and the stamp pad to print the corresponding number of bugs on each page. One note: If insect and spider rubber stamps are unavailable, let each child create bugs using his fingerprints and a fine-line marker.

Ladybug Math

Have a small group of children sit around a table. Place a set of dominoes (removing the zero, eleven and twelve domino) facedown in the center of the table. Then give each child a copy of one of the four playing cards on page 140. Tell a child to turn over one domino. If the number of dots on the domino totals a number on her playing card, have her place the domino over the number. If not, tell her to return the domino facedown on the table. Continue play in the same manner. The game ends when one child covers her entire playing card with dominoes.

Spider Legs

How many legs does a spider have? Eight! Have a small group of children sit around a table. Give each child a black circle to represent a spider's body. Place a large die and a supply of clothespins (spider legs) in the center of the table. In turn, have each child roll the die. The child who rolls the highest number clips the corresponding number of clothespins to her circle. The first child to attach all eight legs to her spider is the winner. To vary the activity, play the game using the lowest number rolled each turn.

LANGUAGE ARTS

Buggy Syllables

Print each of the following words on individual cards and place them in a hat. In turn, have each child draw one card from the hat. Read the word on the card. Tell your children to listen to the number of times you clap your hands as you say each word. Then have them hold up the appropriate number of fingers to indicate the number of syllables.

ant	cricket	grasshopper
tick	firefly	butterfly
moth	stinkbug	ladybug
fly	beetle	dragonfly
wasp	hornet	mosquito
flea	termite	bumblebee
roach	mayfly	katydid

Guess Who

To prepare for this activity, attach pictures of different insects to individual index cards. Print the name of each insect under its picture. Then place the cards inside a bug box or safari hat. Have a student volunteer draw a card from the box. Tell him to describe the insect to the class without naming it. Encourage the child to use words detailing the insect's colors, size, wings, antennae, eyes, and other interesting features. Then have the children guess the name of the insect.

Old Black Fly

The ABC book *Old Black Fly* by Jim Aylesworth describes the many things an old black fly did one day. Each of the 26 events highlights a different letter of the alphabet. Read the story to your children. Then reread the story, stopping after each event to let your children name the words that begin with the particular letter. Write the words on a sheet of chart paper. Later, copy the words on index cards and illustrate each card. Have the children copy the words onto separate sheets of paper and illustrate each page. For younger children, write shorter words on the cards such as *ant, fly, bee,* and *flea.*

Wasps

Print the poem "Wasps" by Dorothy Aldis, from *The Random House Book Of Poetry For Children* selected by Jack Prelutsky, on a sheet of chart paper. Cut out or draw a picture of each thing a wasp likes, such as coffee, syrup, tea, soda, and butter. Glue the pictures on index cards. Attach a small mirror or a piece of aluminum foil to another index card to represent the word *me.* Then place the picture cards, the mirror card, and the chart in a center. Help the children attach the cards to the chart beside the appropriate words and then read the poem aloud.

Ants

Two Bad Ants by Chris Van Allsburg describes a day in the life of two mischievous ants from their perspective. As you read the book to your children, have them name the strange objects encountered by the ants such as "the crystals"; "the giant scoop"; "the hot, brown liquid"; and "the cave." Then ask your children to guess what the ants might call other objects such as a fork, a napkin, and a bar of soap.

Honeybee Hive

Print one uppercase letter on each of several honeybee cutouts. Next staple a large hive cutout to a bulletin board. Print each corresponding lowercase letter on the hive. Attach the honeybees around the hive in random order. Invite student volunteers to attach each bee to the hive next to its corresponding letter.

Be A Butterfly

Where Butterflies Grow by Joanne Ryder is a beautifully illustrated book about the life cycle of a butterfly. Read the book aloud to your children. Then discuss the various stages a caterpillar goes through before becoming a butterfly. Reread the book and let your youngsters act out each event. Begin by asking each child to curl up in a ball to represent the egg and turning off the lights until the caterpillar crawls out into the brightness. Continue the activity until the butterfly emerges from the chrysalis and flies away to look for butterflies like himself.

The Very Hungry Caterpillar

At the beginning of the week, read *The Very Hungry Caterpillar* by Eric Carle. Afterward have your children name the different things eaten by the caterpillar. Then give each child a sheet of paper programmed with the sentence, "On Monday I ate ____________." Ask her to draw a picture of one thing she ate for breakfast or lunch, and then write or dictate the name of the food in the blank. Repeat the activity each day of the unit. Then staple the pages together to create individual books titled "The Very Hungry Girl" or "The Very Hungry Boy." To extend the activity, let each child complete the Saturday and Sunday pages for homework before binding the pages together.

The Old Lady Who Swallowed A Fly

Read aloud *There Was An Old Lady Who Swallowed A Fly* illustrated by Pam Adams. Then collect a stuffed toy or picture representative of each animal in the book. Next, draw a picture of the old lady's head on a sheet of poster board; then cut it out. Also cut a large opening for her mouth. Attach the cutout to a clean wastebasket. Give each child in a small group one of the stuffed animals or pictures. Reread the story and let the youngsters put the animals in the old lady's mouth as they are named.

SCIENCE

Insects

Read the poem "Every Insect" by Dorothy Aldis, from *Animals, Animals* by Eric Carle. Then show your children a large picture of an insect. Point out the six legs, the three body parts *(head, thorax, and abdomen),* and the antennae. Then give each child a copy of the insect reproducible on page 141. Tell her to color the picture, cut around the solid black lines, and glue the three sections to a sheet of construction paper in the correct order.

Helpful And Harmful Insects

Share the facts below with your children; then set up a science center in the classroom where children can identify helpful and harmful insects. Include factual books, pictures, insects in clear plastic containers, and examples of things harmful insects have damaged.

Helpful insects include butterflies, moths, wasps, bees, and others that pollinate flowering plants. These insects also pollinate plants that produce fruits and vegetables such as apples, oranges, and cotton. Ladybugs help farmers by eating harmful insects that destroy crops. Silkworms are important because they make the silk we use in clothing such as ties and scarfs. Honeybees produce honey and beeswax. Helpful insects keep the environment clean by eating the remains of dead plants and animals. They are also a source of food for animals such as frogs, fish, and birds.

Harmful insects include the boll weevil, which damages cotton, the corn ear worm, which attacks corn, the Japanese beetle, which eats the leaves and fruits of plants, and the Hessian fly, which destroys wheat. Other harmful insects can destroy items in our homes. For example, clothes moths and carpet beetles eat holes in things made of fabric or fur; silverfish ruin books; termites destroy wooden beams and flooring; and cockroaches, ants, and flies spoil food. Insects such as biting flies and mosquitoes inject a poison into our skin that causes itching and soreness.

Spiders

Show your children a large picture of a spider and ask them to tell why a spider is not an insect. (Spiders have eight legs, two body parts, and no wings or antennae.) Next give each child a copy of the spider reproducible on page 141. Have him color the picture, cut around the solid black lines, and glue the sections to a sheet of construction paper in the correct order.

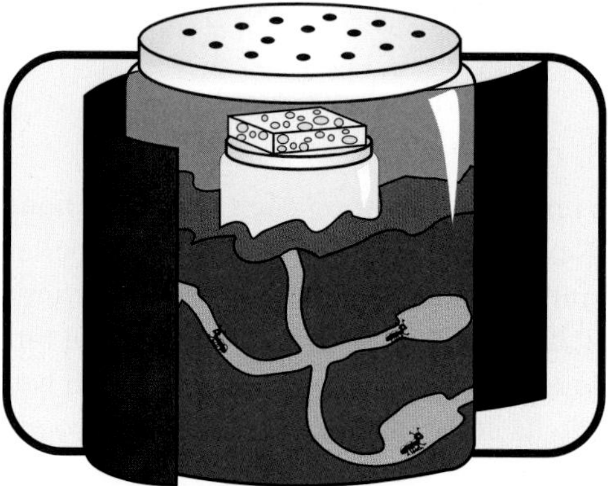

Build An Ant Colony

Help students observe the fascinating world of ants by building a classroom ant colony. (Discourage students from collecting ants at home, as many ants bite.) Follow these steps; then have students record or draw their observations in science journals.

1. Place a small plastic jar (with the lid screwed on) inside a large, lidded jar.
2. Poke very small holes (smaller than an ant) in the large jar's lid.
3. Find an ant hill or a place with loose soil. Use a small shovel to gently dig up the ants and soil. Be sure that you include a queen in your colony. The queen ant is larger than the other ants.
4. Put the soil and ants in the large jar in the space surrounding the smaller jar.
5. Cover the jar with black paper so that the ants will tunnel close to the glass. Remove the paper only during observation periods.
6. Show students how to feed the ants periodically with very small bread crumbs, birdseed, or other small pieces of food. Keep a damp sponge on top of the small jar at all times.
7. Have students observe the ants often and answer questions such as the following:
   - How do the ants spend their time?
   - Do the ants seem to communicate with each other? How?
   - How do ants carry food?

SOCIAL STUDIES

Insect Jobs

Social insects, such as all ants, many bees, and all termites, live in organized communities in which members have specialized jobs. For example, the queen in these colonies lays the eggs. The workers have many different tasks. Some care for the young. Others guard and defend the colony. Others clean and enlarge the nest, and some search for food. Discuss the jobs of social insects with your children. Then discuss various jobs of workers within the school such as the principal, teacher, custodian, nurse, secretary, librarian or media specialist, and cafeteria worker. Ask the children to describe each person's job. Then invite each of these people to visit your classroom and talk about his or her duties and responsibilities.

Plan Ahead

Read aloud "The Grasshopper And The Ant" from *The Classic Treasury of Aesop's Fables* illustrated by Don Daily. Discuss how the hardworking ant worked all summer to save food for the winter and the lazy grasshopper only hopped, leaped, and sang. Then talk about ways we prepare for the future such as freezing and canning food, saving money in the bank, and storing seasonal clothes. If desired, list students' responses on a chart like the one shown below.

PLAN AHEAD

Food	Clothes	Shelter	Heat	Money
canning	storing seasonal clothes	add insulation	wood	savings account
freezing				budget

Pest Control Expert

Invite a pest control expert to visit your classroom. Ask him to bring examples of harmful insects and some of the items they have damaged. Also have him describe the methods he uses to control insects.

Beekeeper

Invite a beekeeper to visit your classroom. Ask him to bring his smoker, hive tools, and special clothing he wears to protect himself from stings. Have him describe the various parts of the hive, then discuss the method he uses for extracting honey from it.

ART

Hairy Spider

Use a marker to draw the outline of a spider on a sheet of paper. Make several copies of the outline on fluorescent paper. Ask a small group of children to sit around a table. Give each child a copy of the spider and a sheet of black construction paper. Have him tear the black paper into small pieces and glue the pieces to the spider's body and legs. Then have him glue eight small pieces of red construction paper to the spider's head to create the eyes. Cut around the spider, leaving a border of fluorescent paper around the edge. Attach the completed spiders to a bulletin board or a string web.

Bug Or Spider Hats

Let each child create a hat representative of her favorite insect or spider. Cut a wide strip of paper to fit around her head. Then let her use markers, paint, and paper scraps to decorate the strip. Encourage her to include features such as eyes, antennae, and wings (for an insect) or eyes (for a spider) on the hat. Next have her fan-fold thin strips of paper to create the legs (six for an insect or eight for a spider). Staple the legs to the hat. Then staple the hat together so it fits the child's head.

Bug Box

Give each child a round oatmeal box and a sheet of construction paper. Let him use paint or markers to decorate the paper. Then help him glue the paper around the outside of the oatmeal box. Cut a hole in the side of the box. Cover the hole with a piece of cellophane and cut slits in the lid. Attach a yarn handle to the lid and place it on the oatmeal box. Then take your youngsters on a hunt for insects they can place in their bug boxes.

Butterfly

Invite each child to create a colorful butterfly with a sheet of construction paper, tempera paint, and plastic spoons. Fold sheets of paper in half and give one to each child. Have her unfold the paper and spoon drops of tempera paint along the fold line. Then have her refold the paper, rub it with the palm of her hand from the fold to the edge, and then open the paper again. If more color is needed, add drops of tempera paint to the paper and repeat the procedure. After the paint is dry, refold the paper and cut it into the shape of a butterfly. Mount the butterflies on construction paper or attach them to a bulletin board.

SNACK

Spider Cookies

Give each child two sandwich cookies. Have her insert eight pretzel sticks into the cream of one cookie to create the spider's legs. Next tell her to place the cookies side by side. Then tell her to place eight mini chocolate chips on the cookie with the legs to create the spider eyes.

CULMINATING ACTIVITY

Butterfly Garden

Select an area on the school grounds suitable for a flower garden. Let your children plant a variety of fragrant flowers that attract butterflies such as creeping phlox, primroses, candytuft, purple or crimson aubrieta, yellow alyssum, bluebells, sweet rocket, scabiosa, and thistles.

Insects and Spiders Playing Cards

Use with "Ladybug Addition" on page 133.

2	5
8	1
9	10
6 TEC61182	TEC61182 4
4	8
7	2
9	6
5 TEC61182	TEC61182 3

Use with "Insects" and "Spiders" on page 136.

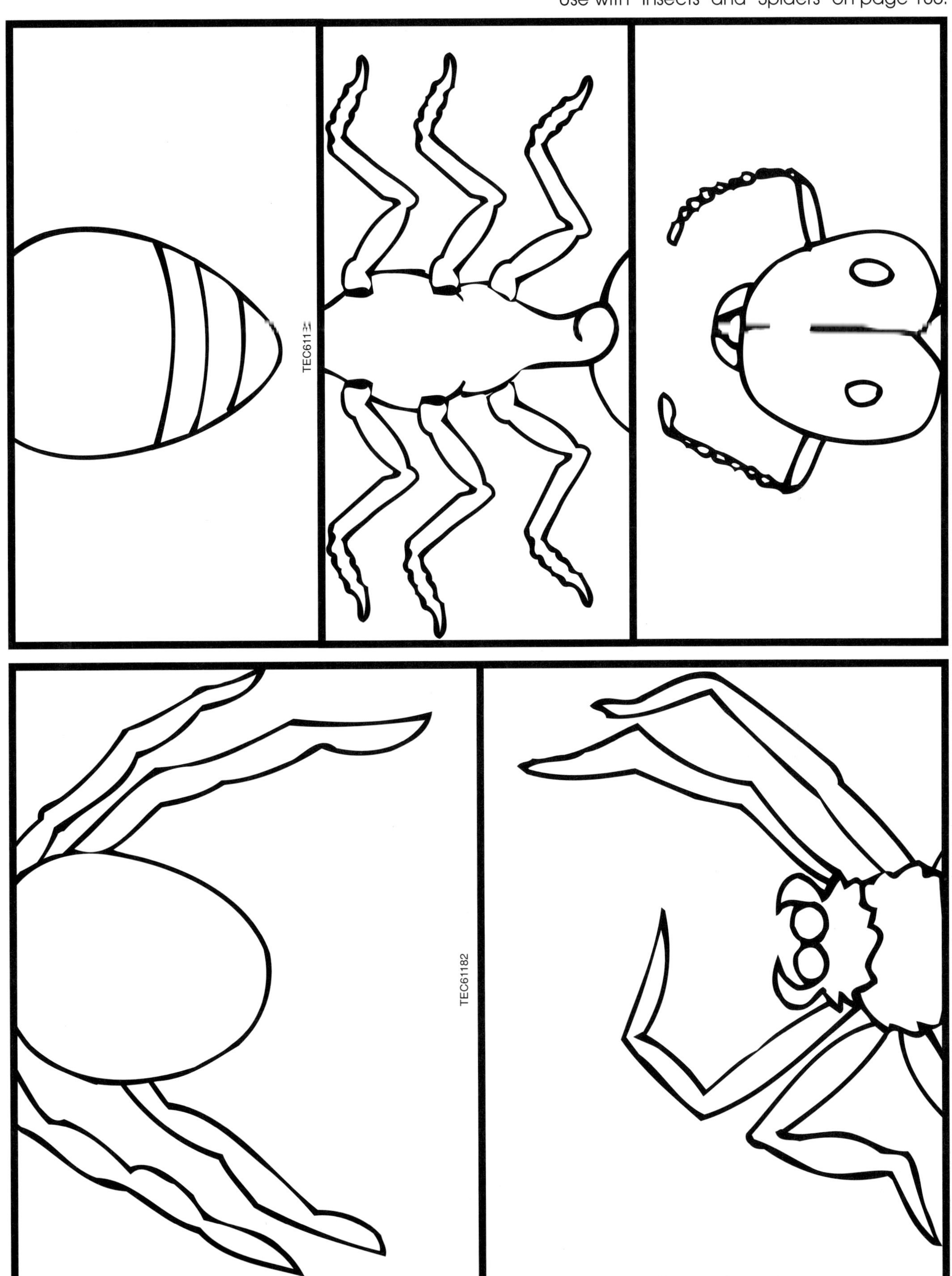

Under The Sea

Dive into adventures exploring the mysteries of the sea! Create a seaside environment in your classroom that will invite children to discover a world of sand, shells, and sea life.

MATH

Schools Of Fish

Seat a small group of students at a table. Give each child 12 Goldfish crackers. Assist children in following the directions below to create different schools of fish. Be sure to tell children that they will not use all of the crackers for each direction.

Make a row with four.	Make two rows of two.
Make a row with two.	Make one row of ten.
Make a row with five.	Make two rows of four.
Make a row with seven.	Make three rows of three.

Sizing Up Shells

Place a bucket filled with a variety of shells in a center. Invite the children to sort the shells by size, placing the small, medium, and large shells on three separate trays. Finally have the children use a set of scales to compare the shells. They may, for example, put a large shell on one side of the scales and see how many small shells they need to put on the other side to balance the scales.

Treasure Chest

Decorate a large shoebox with a lid so it resembles a treasure chest. Then place an assortment of cereal, colored macaroni, and several pipe cleaners in the box. Have children use the items in the box to make bracelets with various patterns.

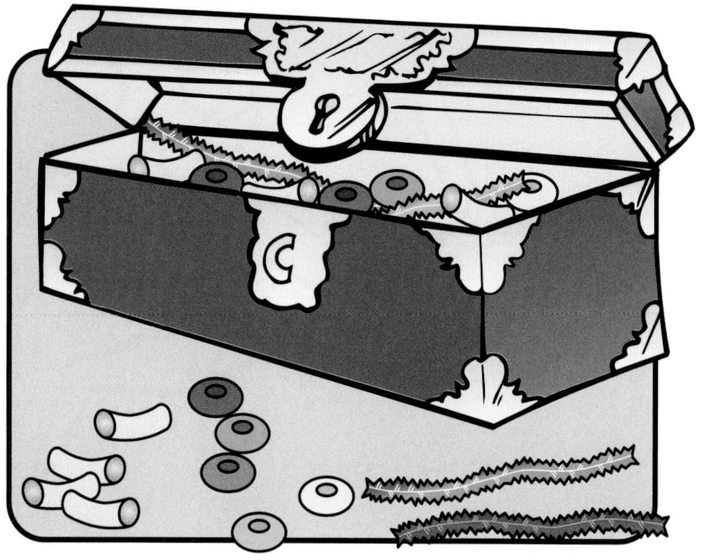

Sailing, Sailing

Place several containers of various sizes (that a toy boat would comfortably fit into), a measuring cup, and a toy boat in a center. Invite a child in the center to put the boat in one of the containers. Then predict how many cups of water it will take to make the boat rise to the top of the container. Once the predictions have been made, have the children pour water by the cupful into the container to see how many are needed. Ask the youngsters to repeat the procedure using the other containers.

Buckets Of Shells

Collect ten sand buckets and number them one to ten. Put the buckets and a container of at least 55 craft foam shell cutouts in a center. Instruct the children to count out the appropriate number of shells and place them in each bucket.

Buried Treasure

Place several shoeboxes filled with sand on a table. Bury several plastic animals or cars in the boxes. Assemble a small group of children around the table. Give each of them a shoebox and tell them that the boxes contain buried treasure. You may also say how many pieces of buried treasure each of the boxes contains and have children hunt until all of the pieces are found.

Goldfish Arithmetic

Begin by cutting a piece of blue tagboard into several strips. Write a different number on each strip; then attach a corresponding number of white circles (bubbles) to each strip. Place the strips in a center along with a bowl of Goldfish crackers. Tell the children to count the corresponding number of crackers and place each one on the strip near a bubble. Invite the children to eat the crackers when they are finished.

Goldfish Cracker Predicting

Fill a large container with an assortment of pretzel, cheese, and plain Goldfish crackers. Ask each child to estimate how many crackers are in the container. Write his name and estimation on a sheet of paper. Then have each child fill a small paper cup with crackers from the container and sit in a small group. Have him sort and count the various kinds of Goldfish crackers. List the categories on a large graph. Help the children in each group count the total number of crackers in each category. Then write the totals on the graph. Add the numbers in each category together. Then add the totals together to determine the number of Goldfish crackers in the container. See whose estimates were the closest.

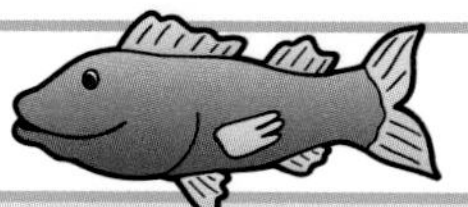

LANGUAGE ARTS

Sand Writing

Write several letters of the alphabet on individual cards. Have each child in a small group pick a letter and trace over it using glue. Then have each child place her letter card inside a box lid. Let the child sprinkle sand over the letter until it is covered completely. Finally have the child lift the letter card out of the lid and carefully shake off the excess sand so that only the letter is covered. When the glue dries, the child can run her fingers over the sand letter to feel its shape. To vary this activity, use each child's name or simple sight words.

Silent Reading

Set up a reading corner in your classroom complete with beach towels and beach bags filled with books about the sea. Allow small groups of children to visit the corner at various times during the week.

Fishing For Letters

Create a fishing game by making several copies of the fish pattern (see page 150) on bright-colored construction paper. Write a different letter, or a sight word, on the back of each fish. Cut them out and attach a jumbo paper clip to each of their mouths. Secure the paper clip with tape.

To make the fishing pole, attach a piece of string to a pole and tie a magnet to the end of the string. Then place the fish on the floor so the letters or words are facedown, and have a small group of children stand in a circle around them. Have children take turns catching fish by holding the fishing pole over a fish so that the magnet touches the paper clip. Once a child catches a fish, have him read what is written on the back. If correct, he keeps the fish. If not, he puts it back. For an added challenge, have children who have caught alphabet fish place them in alphabetical order. Have those who caught sight-word fish try to make simple sentences using some of the words.

A House For Hermit Crab

Read aloud Eric Carle's *A House For Hermit Crab.* Have the children name the things that Hermit Crab gathered to decorate his shell, listing the names in order on chart paper. Once the list is complete, give each child a picture of Hermit Crab (see page 151). Invite children to color the picture and decorate it any way they wish. Have children share their creations with the class. Then bind the papers together in a class book.

Wishes

Read aloud *The Magic Fish* adapted by Freya Littledale. Have your students discuss the foolish wishes made by the fisherman and his wife. Then ask them to think of wise wishes the pair could have made. Once the discussion is over, give each child a piece of paper that has been folded in half lengthwise. Have him draw a picture of something that would be a foolish wish on one half of the paper and something that would be a wise wish on the other half. Invite him to share his two wishes with the other children.

The Bottom Of The Sea

Lead your children in singing "There's A Hole In The Bottom Of The Sea" from the CD *Disney's Silly Songs.* Then have your youngsters say each of the things named in the song that are at the bottom of the sea. Next place a picture of each thing in random order in front of the class. Have student volunteers place the pictures in the correct sequence. Finally ask a small group of children to stand in a line. Give each child one of the pictures. Then lead the class in singing the song again. Have each child in the small group hold up her picture when it is mentioned in the song.

Tongue Twisters

Print the tongue twister "She sells seashells by the seashore" on a sheet of chart paper. Read the tongue twister aloud to your class. Then have your children repeat it with you. Repeat the procedure with other tongue twisters. Then discuss reasons why this type of poem is so difficult to say.

Rhyming Book

Have your children think of words that rhyme with *shell.* Print the words on chart paper as they are dictated by the children. Next give each child three seashell cutouts. Ask her to choose three of the rhyming words and draw a picture of each on one of the sheets of paper. Help her label each picture. Then bind the pages inside a shell-shaped cover.

SCIENCE

Seawater Jar

Give each child in a small group a clear plastic jar. Have him place a shell, some rocks, and a handful of sand in his jar. Then pour water in the jar until it is approximately three-fourths full. Secure the lid tightly and tell him to shake the jar vigorously. Finally have him place the jar on a table and watch carefully to see what will happen.

Beautiful Shells

Put several shells in small shoeboxes, and place them in a center. Give one box to each child at the center. Tell the children to look at their shells very carefully, observing each shell's unique features. Then assist each child in completing a recording sheet (see page 150). Have him share his results with the others in the group.

Fresh Water And Salt Water

Pour two cups of tap water in a small, deep, clear container. In a similar container, pour two cups of very warm water and add six to seven tablespoons of salt. Stir until the salt dissolves and let the water cool slightly. Place a raw egg in the container of tap water and it will sink. Then place the same egg in the container of salt water and it will float.

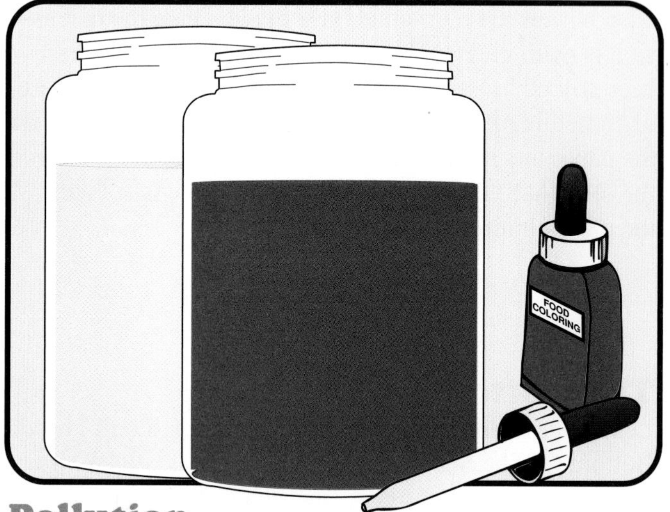

Pollution

Prepare a demonstration to illustrate the effects of pollution. First fill two plastic jars with clear tap water. Show the jars of water to your students. Then pour several "pollutants" into one jar. Ask the children which of the two jars they would want to live in if they were fish. Let this simple activity be a springboard for discussing how oceans become polluted and what we can do to help make them clean.

Animal Differences

Talk about the differences between animals that live on land and those that live in water. Then have your children look through old magazines and cut out pictures of both types of animals. Glue the pictures on two separate posters.

SOCIAL STUDIES

Class Aquarium

Enjoy the beauty of the sea in your own classroom. Set up a classroom aquarium. Provide the tank and filtering device, along with items such as seashells, plastic seaweed, fish, and fish food. Assign a different helper to feed the fish and clean the aquarium each week.

Sea Jobs

The sea provides many jobs, such as those of divers, fishermen, lifeguards, marine biologists, treasure hunters, sailors, truckers, and restaurant workers. Have your children name sea-related jobs, and list each one on a sheet of chart paper. Then let each child choose one job, draw a picture to illustrate it, and write or copy the job name under the picture. Bind the pages together to create a class book titled "Sea Jobs."

Endangered Species

Read aloud *Humphrey, The Lost Whale: A True Story* by Wendy Tokuda and Richard Hall. Talk about why the humpback whale is considered an endangered species. Then describe the steps being taken to preserve these valuable creatures.

Swimmy

Read aloud *Swimmy* by Leo Lionni. Ask your children to describe how the school of small fish solved a very big problem. Discuss the benefits of working cooperatively. Then have your youngsters work together to create an under-the-sea mural. Draw the ocean floor on the bottom of a large sheet of blue paper. Divide the class into small groups. Give each group a pattern for a starfish, fish, crab, sea anemone, or sea horse to trace and cut out. Then let the children work as a class to attach the various pieces to the sheet of background paper.

ART

Crayon Resist

A successful crayon-resist painting depends upon the following things: the paper used should be white or light-colored construction paper, and the crayons must be very waxy (Prang crayons work well) and applied very heavily to the paper.

With these recommendations in mind, set up a center in the classroom where children can create crayon-resist paintings of life under the sea. Begin by allowing the children time to color their pictures. Then give each child a paintbrush and a small jar of blue, water-diluted tempera paint. Have each child dip her brush into the jar and carefully paint over the entire surface of her picture. The paint will color the areas of the paper not covered with crayon and will help create the illusion of an underwater scene.

One final note: As the paint begins to dry, the paper will curl. To remedy this situation, allow the paint to dry completely and place the paintings under heavy books to help flatten them.

Plaster Relief

An attractive plaster relief can be made using a variety of seashells, several pie tins, and moist earth clay. First give each child a pie tin and a ball of clay. Have her place the clay in the bottom of the tin, piece by piece, until the bottom is filled to a one-inch thickness. Next have her create impressions in the clay and pour liquid plaster over it until an approximate one-inch thickness is obtained. To make a hanger for the sculpture, insert a bent paper clip into the wet plaster. Finally allow the plaster to dry completely, and carefully separate it from the pie tin and the clay.

Diorama

Ask each child to bring a large shoebox lid from home. Then, in a small group, have each child paint the inside of her lid white. When the paint has dried completely, have her use markers to draw the ocean floor and some seaweed inside the lid. Next place a container of plastic fish, crabs, starfish, and sea horses in the center, and invite each child to choose four or five. Have her glue the objects to the sea scene. Then cover the lid with blue-tinted plastic wrap and tape the plastic to the back of the lid.

SNACK

Sand Cups

2 cups cold milk
1 package (4-serving size) Jell-O vanilla-flavor instant pudding
1 tub (8 oz.) Cool Whip whipped topping, thawed
1 package (12 oz.) vanilla wafers, crushed
8–10 (7 oz.) clear plastic cups

Pour milk into large bowl. Add pudding mix. Beat with whisk until well blended, about 1 to 2 minutes. Let stand 5 minutes. Stir in whipped topping and half of crushed cookies. Place 1 tablespoon of crushed cookies into each cup. Fill cups three-fourths full with pudding mixture. Top with remaining crushed cookies. Refrigerate for 1 hour. Decorate as desired. Yield: 8–10 sand cups.

CULMINATING ACTIVITY

Beach Party

Send home a letter with each child explaining that a class beach party will be held on the last day of the Under the Sea unit. Encourage every child to bring to school an item that he might normally take with him to the beach (sand bucket, small plastic shovel, beach towel, sunglasses, etc.).

On the day of the party, let the children wear their beach apparel, and have several outside beach activities planned. For example, you may have the class participate in beach-ball relay races, sand castle–building competition, or target practice with spray bottles of water. Afterward, when you bring the children back into the classroom, allow them to rest on their beach towels, and play beach music in the background. Finally let the children enjoy a "sand cup" Jell-O pudding snack (see the recipe at left).

Fish Pattern

Use with "Fishing For Letters" on page 144.

Name ______________________ Observing shells

Seashells

	Yes	No
1. Did you see a shell with purple on it?	❑	❑
2. Did you see a shell that was shiny?	❑	❑
3. Did you see a shell that had ridges?	❑	❑
4. Did you see a shell with points?	❑	❑
5. Did you hear a sound in a shell?	❑	❑

 Note to the Teacher: Use with "Beautiful Shells" on page 146.

Note to the teacher: Use with "A House For Hermit Crab" on page 144.

Zoo Animals

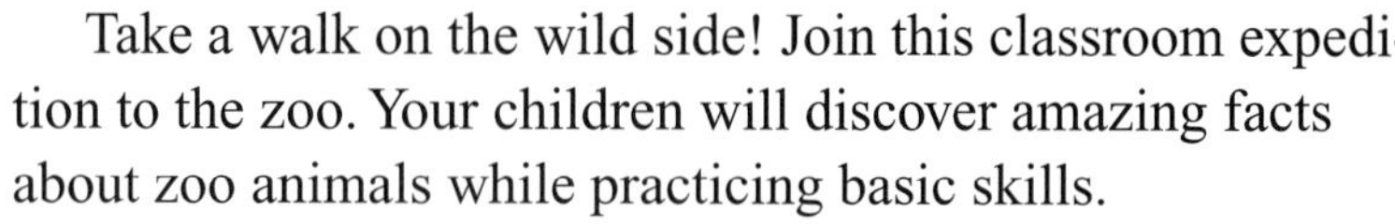

Take a walk on the wild side! Join this classroom expedition to the zoo. Your children will discover amazing facts about zoo animals while practicing basic skills.

MATH

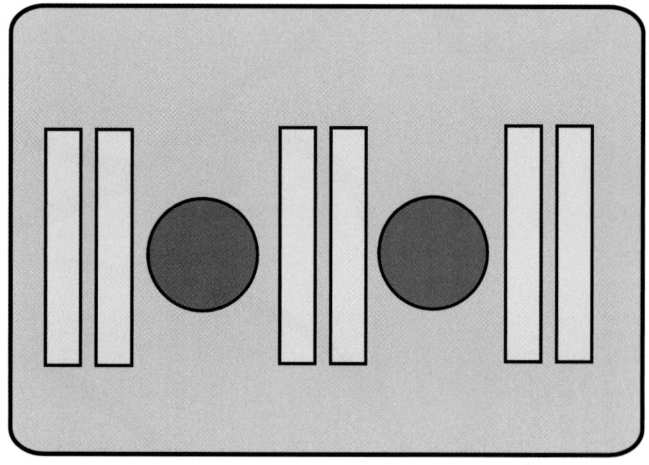

Sorting Zoo Animals

Place various plastic animals of all types in a basket. Include dinosaurs, farm animals, pets, and zoo animals. Instruct a small group of children to sort the animals into two groups: zoo animals and animals that don't live in a zoo. Then have them count the number of animals in both groups and tell which has more.

Spots And Stripes

Many wild animals have special markings such as spots and stripes to help them hide in their natural environments. Place several paper circles and strips in a center. Have the children make several different patterns with the two shapes.

Long Legs

The giraffe is the tallest of all the animals. It gets its height from its legs, which are six feet long. Draw a six-foot giraffe leg. Attach it to a wall in the classroom. Have each child stand beside the leg. Mark his height with a piece of tape. Write the child's name on the tape. Then compare his height with that of the giraffe's leg and his classmates.

Animal Crackers

How many lions are there in a box of animal crackers? How many zebras? To determine the answers to these and other questions have your children sort, count, and graph a large box of animal crackers. Make a class graph by attaching an example of each animal cracker on the left-hand side of a grid. Then divide the remaining crackers into individual cups. Give each child a cup. Ask her to sort the animal crackers by kind. Then record the information on the class graph by coloring in a square beside each animal cracker. Finally total the number of animal crackers graphed.

Animal Count

To prepare for this activity, place a container of plastic zoo animals along with several containers labeled as shown in a center. Have the children sort the zoo animals into the labeled containers. Then have them count the number of animals in each container.

1, 2, 3

Read aloud *1, 2, 3 To The Zoo: A Counting Book* by Eric Carle. Discuss the sequence of the numbers in the book. Next give each of ten volunteers a number card between one and ten. Have the children stand in random order. Then instruct the group to arrange themselves in the correct numerical order. Finally place three number cards such as 3, 4, and 6 in a pocket chart. Ask your children to tell which numbers are missing. Repeat the activity using different sets of numbers.

LANGUAGE ARTS

I Like...

Read the poem "Giraffes" by Mary Ann Hoberman from *Animals Animals* by Eric Carle. Discuss the many reasons the author gives for liking giraffes. Then ask each child to name a zoo animal and tell one reason for liking it. For example, "I like monkeys because they swing by their tails." Write each sentence on a sheet of chart paper as it is dictated. Then copy the sentences on individual sheets of paper. Let each child illustrate his sentence. Then bind the papers together to create a class book titled "We Like Zoo Animals."

Describing Zoo Animals

Cut out pictures of zoo animals from magazines such as *Ranger Rick* or *National Geographic*. Glue the pictures on individual sheets of paper. Let each child choose one picture and think of words to describe it. Write the words on the paper. Then bind the papers together to create a class book titled "Children's Zoo."

Zoo Animals' Names

Your children will practice letter-recognition skills while spelling zoo animal names. Give each pair of children in a small group a set of lowercase letter cards. Tell each pair to spread out the cards on the floor or tabletop so they can see each card. Then spell a zoo animal's name using uppercase letters in a pocket chart. Have the children work together to spell the same name using the lowercase letters. Continue in the same manner using zoo animal names such as *lion, seal, zebra, monkey, tiger, leopard, bear, camel, python, walrus,* and *flamingo.*

Python Rhyming Words

Ask your children to help you make lists of rhyming words on chart paper. Then give each child a copy of the python reproducible on page 159. Have him color the python's head and tail and cut out both shapes. Then give him a piece of paper that has been fan-folded (as shown). Instruct him to choose rhyming words from the list and copy each word in a section of the folded paper. Tell him to glue the python's head to the top of the paper and the tail to the bottom.

Rebus Book

Give each child a copy of the reproducible on page 160. Have her cut apart the rebus sentences on the solid black lines and then cut the pictures from the end of each strip. Next have her glue each sentence to the bottom of a sheet of paper, and then glue a picture to each shaded box. Ask her to illustrate each sentence. Then bind the pages inside a bright-colored, construction paper cover to create an individual book titled "The Zoo Book."

Zoo Box

Paint a large cardboard box so it resembles a cage. Then place several objects in the box. (The name of each object should begin with a different beginning sound.) Take the objects out of the box one at a time and place them on the floor. As you do this, ask your children to name each object and its beginning sound.

Animal ABC

Your youngsters will want to play this card game again and again. To prepare for the game, write the names of several zoo animals on separate cards, and then attach a picture of each animal to the card. Shuffle the cards and place them facedown in the center of a table. Ask a small group of children to sit around the table. Instruct each child to take one card from the top of the stack, show it to the others, and name the animal. The child with the letter that comes first in the alphabet may take the others' cards. Have the children repeat the procedure until all the cards have been played.

SCIENCE

Observing The Unusual

Collect several pictures of unusual zoo animals such as the sloth, the platypus, and the lemur. Invite children to observe a picture and describe the animal. Make a list of the observations as they are shared. Then repeat the activity with the remaining pictures.

Zoo Food

Feeding the zoo animals is a very important job for the zookeeper. Each animal must be given the correct amount of food that contains the right mixture of nourishing ingredients. For more information about feeding zoo animals, read *Lunch at the Zoo: What Animals Eat and Why* by Joyce Altman. Write the names of several zoo animals on chart paper. Under each name, write examples of foods used to feed the animal. Then prepare a zoo snack for your children with a food from each of the following categories (*meat*—pepperoni, *plants*—parsley or lettuce, *mixed*—Cheerios).

Zoo Babies

To introduce your children to baby zoo animals, read the book *The Baby Zoo* by Bruce McMillan. Then ask your children to help you list the baby animal names such as *calf, cub,* and *kid.* Have your youngsters think of other baby animals that have the same names and add them to the list. Finally make a book of baby animal names by writing each one on a sheet of paper. Then have your children draw or glue pictures of baby animals with that name on each paper.

What Do You Hear?

Read aloud *Polar Bear, Polar Bear, What Do You Hear?* by Bill Martin Jr. Then ask your children to close their eyes. Make several sounds such as dropping a book, clapping your hands, and crumpling a sheet of paper. Ask your children to identify each sound. Then ask each child to think of one sound she could make. Have her make the sound and ask the other children to guess what it is.

SOCIAL STUDIES

Field Trip

Plan a field trip to a local zoo. If a zoo is not located near your school, let your children watch a video or DVD showing zoo life. Afterward discuss the duties and responsibilities of various zoo workers such as the veterinarian, the dietitian, the groundskeepers, and the concession workers. Ask each child to draw a picture of one worker performing his job at the zoo. Display the pictures on a bulletin board.

Locate On A Map

Many zoo animals lived in faraway lands before coming to live in the zoo. Attach pictures of common zoo animals—such as an elephant, a giraffe, and a chimpanzee—around a world map. Locate the natural habitat of each animal on the map. Match it to the picture of the animal with a piece of yarn. Display the map in the classroom for the duration of the unit.

Adopt An Animal

Help your children become better acquainted with a desert tortoise, a warthog, or a screech owl. Many zoos have an adopt-an-animal program that will provide your children with learning opportunities throughout the school year. Check local zoos or nature science centers for program information.

ART

Zebra Stripes

Create an attractive zebra stripes design by printing black on white. To prepare for the activity, make a printing block for each child in a small group. Wrap jute twine around a wooden block and tie in the back. (Make sure there is space between the strands of twine.) Tell each child to dip her block into a tray of black paint. Then have her press it on a sheet of white construction paper to create the stripes. Instruct her to repeat the procedure several times. When the paint is dry, mount the print on a black sheet of construction paper. To vary the activity, use white tempera paint and black paper.

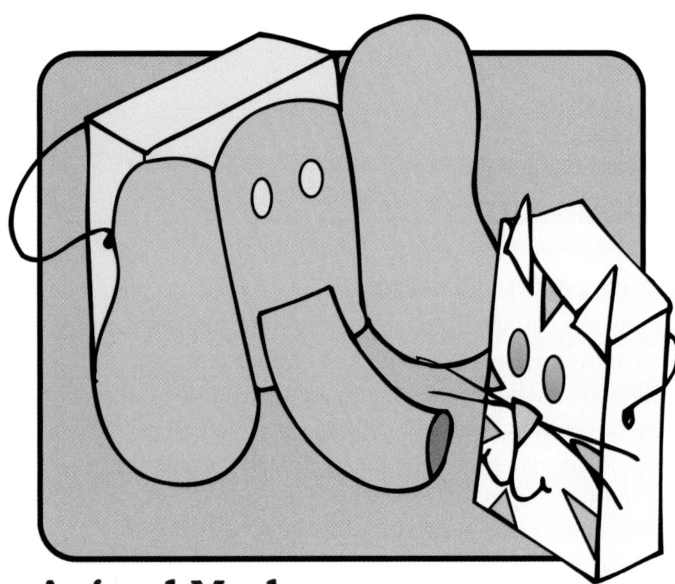

Animal Masks

Let each child create an animal mask using construction paper, scissors, markers, yarn, and a cereal box. Collect a quantity of cereal boxes. Cut off the back and the bottom side of each box. Next give each child a sheet of construction paper. Have her draw the outline of an animal's face on the paper and cut it out. Tell her to use paper scraps and markers to decorate the face. Then mount it on the front of a cereal box as shown. Cut the front of the box to match the shape of the face. Cut holes for the eyes. Then punch a hole in each side of the box and thread a piece of yarn through each hole. Fit the mask on the child's head and tie the yarn in the back.

SNACK

Python Cookies

Soften a tube of slice-and-bake cookie dough. Roll the cookie dough into a ball. Add ten drops of food coloring and mix. (The food coloring will not mix thoroughly, creating stripes in the cookies.) Roll out the cookie dough into a ¼-inch-wide strand. Cut the strand into 6-inch pieces. Shape each piece into an *s*-shape. Press in two small candies for the eyes. Bake according to package directions.

CULMINATING ACTIVITY

Zany Zoo

Invite each child to participate in the creation of a zany zoo. Ask her to sculpt a zoo animal from a ball of clay. Let the clay figure harden. Then have her paint it an unusual color. Display the zany zoo in the classroom, media center, or other prominent school location.

Python Patterns

Use with "Python Rhyming Words" on page 155.

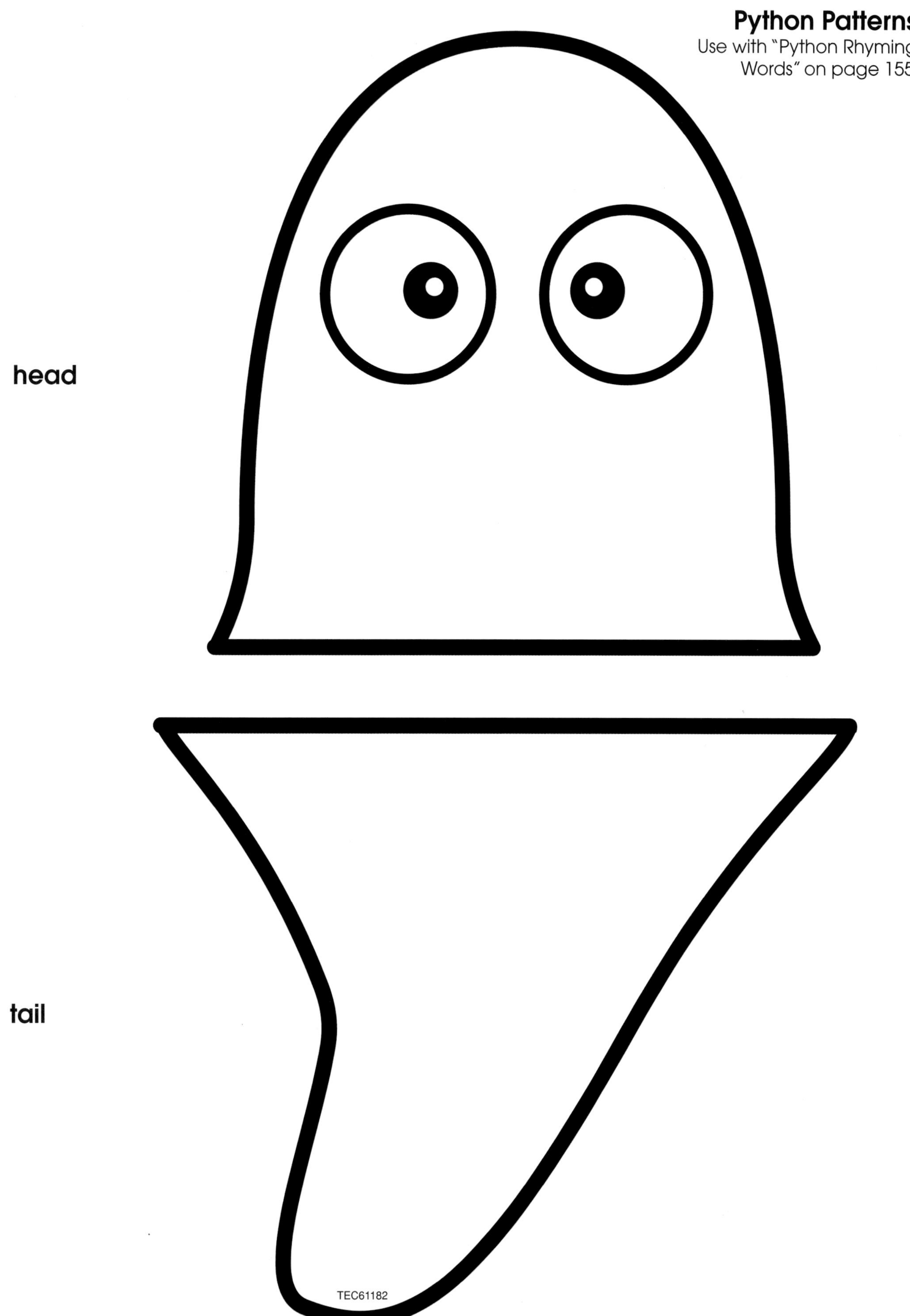

Rebus Sentences

Use with "Rebus Book" on page 155.

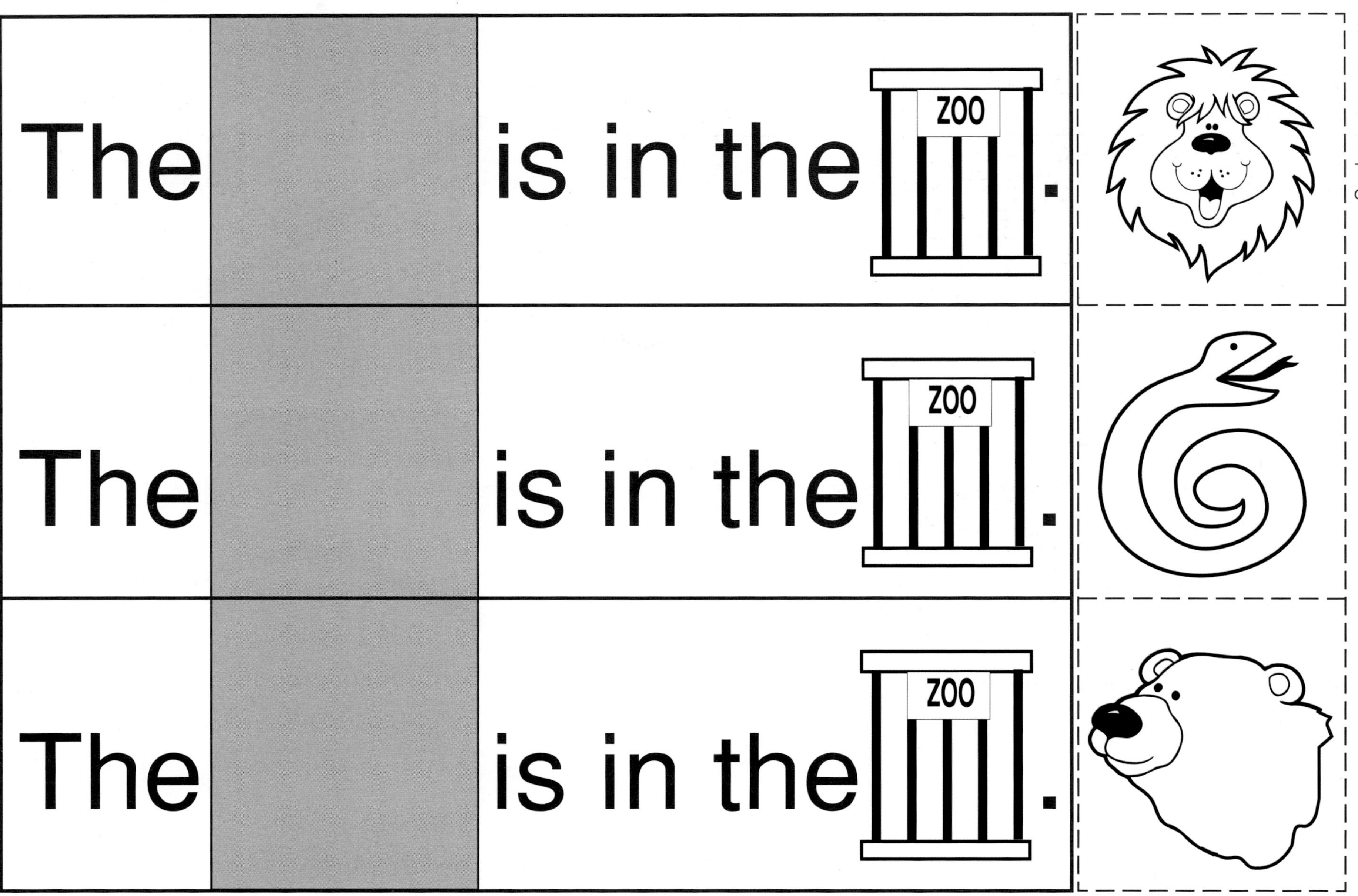